The Bride's Book of Flower Arrangement

PLATE I *(Frontispiece).* Two calla lilies and one calla leaf in a golden-brown glass vase. Water barely covers the glass balls, keeping the emphasis on the vase.

The Bride's Book of Flower Arrangement

by Caroline B. Whitaker

photographs by Miki Takagi

CHARLES E. TUTTLE COMPANY
Rutland, Vermont & Tokyo, Japan

Representatives

For Continental Europe:
BOXERBOOKS, INC., *Zurich*

For the British Isles:
PRENTICE-HALL INTERNATIONAL, INC., *London*

For Canada:
HURTIG PUBLISHERS, *Edmonton*

For Australasia:
PAUL FLESCH & CO., PTY. LTD.,
c/o BOOKWISE AUSTRALIA
104 Sussex Street, Sydney

Published by the Charles E. Tuttle Company, Inc.
of Rutland, Vermont & Tokyo, Japan
with editorial offices at
Suido 1-chome, 2-6, Bunkyo-ku, Tokyo

Copyright in Japan, 1975
by Charles E. Tuttle Co., Inc.

Library of Congress Catalog Card No. 74-83392
International Standard Book No. 0-8048 1143-1

First printing, 1975

Printed in Japan

To all brides

*May your marriage be
as happy and fulfilling as
mine has been*

Table of Contents

List of Illustrations

FIGURES

Acknowledgments

Several writing years have gone into the making of this book, which still would not have been possible without the cooperation of many people.

To Grand Master Sofu Teshigahara of the Sogetsu School of Japan, for his wonderful inspiration and invaluable aid, my heartfelt thanks. To Kasumi Teshigahara, individual thanks for all her help. To the staff and personnel of the Sogetsu School, my warmest appreciation for their unstinting efforts to help me in every way.

To my husband with his continuing, careful, loving assistance, I offer public thanks. I marvel at his fortitude.

A very special thanks to my many students throughout the world whom I couldn't begin to name. With their constant encouragement and faith, I didn't dare let down.

My gratitude to Miki Takagi, whose skill in flower photography, already world-famous, was invaluable to me. Special thanks, too, to my Filipino artist, Cesar A. Arcilla, so perceptive in catching my wishes for special effect in sketches.

Thanks to the staff of the Charles E. Tuttle Co. for their forbearance with a "first book" author.

Last, but far from least, to my special friend and teacher, Mrs. Shuko Ochiai, whose house has been my second home, and whose help is always given with affection and boundless patience.

1

Character Flower Arranging

Flower arrangements are a gift of beauty from you to your husband and your friends. Each time you arrange, you create an "original," never done before, never to be repeated. The varied charm, radiance, and elegance of flowers give you a direct route to beauty for your new home.

In addition, when the imagination is stirred, arrangements can be creative. To inspire your fancy, the spirit of Ikebana, Japanese flower arranging, is introduced. Why Japanese flower arranging? Because the Japanese are the only people in the world who include flower arranging as a mandatory educational course for their young people, both men and women. Highly prized wedding gifts for Japanese brides are flower containers, especially those that are family heirlooms.

Discussions with many brides on the problems of flower arranging reveal that they have budget limitations, time limitations, and limitations of space in new living quarters. These problems can be solved with "Character flower arranging," a term you will come to know intimately in the pages to follow.

Solutions to beauty on a budget:

(1) Character arrangements use only a few flowers.
(2) Basic patterns, once arranged, will need only flowers changed.

(3) Special flower material can be made up ahead of time and stored for emergencies, just as food is prepared and frozen.

(4) Suggested arrangements will outlive by two or three times the usual flower arrangement.

(5) Although arrangements in the book are suitable for small rooms, when space is no longer a limiting factor basic styles can be expanded proportionately to the available area.

Creativity in Flower Arranging

A happy solution to creativity in flower arranging is to take a new look at your appraisal of beauty. You have standards already by which you judge beauty. For flower arranging, you may be impressed by the loveliness of the flower petals. Few would question the appeal of pretty flowers, but let's think about expanding the beauty horizon beyond prettiness.

Prettiness may imply only a surface charm. The best example is color. If we carry beauty of color one step beyond the beautiful colors of a rose (or any flower), then, logically, there's beauty in the coloration of mandarin oranges, new maple leaves, eggplant, or a shining brass surface. Couldn't these be added, or substituted, for the color-beauty of a flower?

Consider shape. There's beauty in the shape of pine branches against the sky (or the wall of your home), there's beauty in palm fronds and in massive redwood tree trunks. How about the beauty of spiraled copper wire?

Texture has beauty. You are already familiar with the interesting surface-look of pine cones. What about crisp, shiny magnolia leaves; fresh-flowering, crinkly kale; the rough bark of cedar branches? These are all aesthetically pleasing. So is the golden or copper mesh of kitchen scour-pads. (See tray arrangement, plate 9.)

Plate 9
(p. 50)
Beauty is not bizarre. As the old saying goes, beauty is in

the eye of the beholder. If you wish to expand your own horizon of beauty, apply this criterion to flower-arranging materials and designs. Flower arrangements for any modern bride should be "now" arrangements: provocative, beautiful, interesting to both arranger and viewer. To designate "now" flower design, the term "Character flower arrangement" has been devised.

Character Flower Arrangements

The make-up of a Character flower arrangement is not one flower in a silver jigger, or two roses in a crystal bud vase, or a brass teakettle with masses of yellow daisies. These are all attractive but are not necessarily creative. Character arrangements have one other ingredient besides flower blooms—something for, or with, "character."

"Character" can be anything out of the ordinary: a piece of driftwood, a beautiful rock, a shell, an unusually shaped flower petal, a curved stem of a branch, an interestingly shaped leaf, some sparkling, small glass marbles—like the

Plate 1 (Frontispiece) arrangement in the brown glass vase (plate 1).

You can easily find glass marbles. Notice that in the arrangement they are used to hold the flower material, as well as to add sparkle.

Although the brown glass vase is unusual, any glass container—tall, short, wide-mouthed, tapered or footed— might be used.

For you, the beginner, let me point out two specific details to note in the arrangement: with unadorned glass, the flower material itself acts as decoration; and the glass, although colored, is crystal clear, not opaque or misty. Notice that the glass marbles are translucent and reflect light in a sparkling fashion.

To vary this idea, use a clear white glass with colored marbles. All sea-green, all blue, or layers of different hues in an harmonious pattern may fit a color scheme you have in mind.

You can substitute other flowers in this arrangement, roses for example. Three to five are plenty. Cut the stems to varying lengths, and remove all leaves below the water line. Cut off thorns so that when you insert stems among the marbles the pattern will not be unduly disturbed. If you plan to use your flowers above the rim of the container, slant the stems for a pretty effect. If more greens are needed, do you have fresh parsley or carrot tops?

How are you going to find something out of the ordinary for an original Character arrangement? There are three important aspects to consider: materials; containers; and places to put arrangements—that is, positioning or setting.

Underlying these three points is the guiding spirit of Ikebana. Is an Ikebana different from Western flower arranging? It is. Since our goal is to amalgamate the two for Character arrangements, we must analyze the differences.

The Ikebana Differences

Flower arrangements the world over are used in the home for the simple pleasure of enjoying fresh flowers. In addition, in Japan, an Ikebana is a representation of all nature: one flower is the epitome of all flowers; one branch, of all trees. With today's emphasis on ecology, this viewpoint can be approved and encouraged, but normally Western flower arrangements are used for decoration. They are planned for effects of color, as one element of an integrated decor. Rarely is the flower arrangement the dominant feature of a room.

Without a doubt, an Ikebana is decorative; but it is never an unobtrusive element or merely part of a decorator's plan. Ikebana is the rule in a Japanese household, not the exception, and Japanese housewives shop for food and flowers simultaneously. Ikebana is an integral force in living; it is nature brought into the home. A flower arrangement is almost as common as rice in a Japanese home. One is food for the body; the other is food for the soul.

Many, many schools of Ikebana flourish throughout Japan. Courses are available from kindergarten through graduate school. Business houses and industries hire Ikebana teachers and encourage their employees to study flower arranging on the premises. All Japanese learn some Ikebana; everyone has a rudimentary knowledge of the art and its points of excellence.

When a guest arrives in the home where an Ikebana has been created, the arrangement is deliberately enjoyed, like a prize painting. What do they discuss about an Ikebana? It is admired for any one of a number of qualities:

(1) the design and overall pattern of the flower material
(2) the perceptiveness of the arranger in choosing particular flowers for the guest's personal delight (a mother-in-law may have a special love for carnations)
(3) the arranger's imagination in combining materials (see plate 5)
(4) the arranger's technical skill in mechanics
(5) the perfect harmony of container, flower materials, and setting
(6) the color composition
(7) the arranger's creativity in handling common materials
(8) any other special feature, such as a celebration arrangement

Plate 5 (p. 46)

Another point of difference concerns the flower material used. Here is the area to study closely for Character arrangements. Average flower compositions are frequently restricted to flower blooms. Ikebana creators regard flower blooms mainly as accessories, highlights for the arrangement, just as jewels are a highlight for a beautifully dressed woman.

What do they use in addition to flowers? In general, the greenery of nature: branches of trees, branches of bushes, and large and small individual leaves such as palm fronds, fatsia japonica leaves, New Zealand flax. They use seedpods on branches, chestnut burrs, bittersweet, okra; they use grasses, fresh or dried.

Man-made and abstract materials add interest to modern Ikebana: cork, plastics, acrylics, wire, screening, spools of metal thread, building materials, glass, glass slag, metals of chrome, copper, iron, aluminum. The list is limited only by the arranger's imagination.

Even if you do not wish to consider your arrangements as art creations, using only flowers for decoration might arouse the same monotony to be had in eating fillet of tenderloin (if one had a choice) every day for weeks and weeks. Delicious, but boring. Varying the diet would add zest. Varying the flower-arrangement diet with Character elements can have the same effect: more zest.

Another difference of particular interest is the Ikebana structure. Traditionally, Ikebana are one-sided, front-viewing styles. Generally Western needs are for a centerpiece for the dining table or for the buffet table, an all-around-viewing style. Of course, flower arrangements are used frequently throughout the home in Western countries. Thank goodness.

Historically, Ikebana were placed in the *tokonoma,* a specifically designed floor-to-ceiling niche in a Japanese home. The *tokonoma* displayed family treasures: an incense burner, a celadon bowl, a painted scroll, an Ikebana.

Using the niche for arranging had its advantages since the height, depth, width, background color, and texture of the niche were fixed and, of course, familiar to the arranger. Possibilities for creativity in this specified area may be likened to those of the poet who must put his thought into the highly specialized form of the sonnet, or dactyls, or limericks. Some can; some can't.

Over the years, the Japanese perfected techniques for these front-viewing styles, so that anyone with patience could be taught to make a flower arrangement of intricate perfection. Eventually, this practice resulted in emphasis on technical excellence and a stabilized design. The stabilized design is what modern Ikebana enthusiasts rebelled against, and free style was innovated. The classical tradition is still strong because it's beautiful. Of course, classical techniques remain invaluable.

Some criticism is leveled at Ikebana regarding its front-viewing styling; it isn't versatile. Very true. The Japanese developed the one-sided arrangement because of their close-ness to nature. Nature, herself, is the prime example of the front-viewing syndrome since plants naturally grow toward the sun.

If you consider the matter, we accept it, perhaps sub-consciously, when we settle plants in our gardens or in our homes. We always try to place the "best side" to the front. Remember the care taken to present the best side of the fresh Christmas tree? No plant grows equally beautifully in all directions. Ikebana emphasize this simple truth.

Most artworks have a best view; few are uniformly interesting from all angles. Uniformity of shape, color, form, and texture is avoided. In Western centerpieces uniformity is practiced, but we might consider varying materials for different viewing angles around the table. The Peacock pattern can accomplish this. (See chapter 10, p. 140.)

Lastly, it may be interesting to you to know that the Japanese student learns classical Ikebana through copying a model again and again until he can reproduce it faithfully. Although the word "copy" is in disrepute, copying a fine model is a prime teaching technique in the study of many art forms.

Regardless of whether or not you wish your flower arrangements to be works of art, there are several credit factors to be noted for the copy method. Accurate basic forms are learned. This gives the student a solid foundation of knowledge. Mechanical techniques are acquired that facilitate rapid arranging. The habit of close observation is developed. Most important, self-discipline is learned.

Certainly not to be overlooked is the student's joy in

achieving a beautiful arrangement fairly quickly! Who wouldn't want to try to repeat a success? A foreign art needs many bridges to close the communication gap.

Plate 18
(p. 98) As an experiment, the arrangement in plate 18 has been left incomplete. Something is needed between the massed red berries and the short-needled pine "carpeting." My suggestion is that you copy the arrangement to the best of your ability, then add your own creative touch. To stir your imagination, here are some ideas I thought of using:

(1) three additional tapers in white, cut short
(2) a madonna figure
(3) three cream or white roses, or chrysanthemums
(4) five white freesia, or narcissi
(5) variegated holly branches cut short, not too many

In actuality, as stated earlier, no one can make the same flower arrangement twice, let alone copy one from a picture. There is the simple matter of pristine flower material which no one has used before. There are changes in setting, changes in time, changes in light, different containers, and, most important, a change in arrangers.

For a shortcut to quick flower arranging, as a beginner, try the copy technique to aid in teaching yourself. Incidentally, it is not as easy as it looks. Guiding principles and photographs for inspiration follow.

For creativity, three precepts can be followed. The first two: never underestimate or forget the impact of unusual, or unfamiliar, flower material; second, be aware of the impact of unusual placement of flowers.

My experience with hundreds of students has shown that unfamiliar materials stimulate the arranger's imagination. Unusual material means unusual growth patterns—curious formations in familiar flowers. It can also mean the use of exotica, plant materials from other places. Either unusual materials or unusual placement gives a fillip needed for successful arranging.

The third precept: don't overlook an unusual way to handle common flower material.

It may be hard for you to think right now of a new way to use a tulip. However, someone thought of wetting fingers and gently turning the petals almost inside out to create a beautiful, wide-spread, "new-look" tulip.

Plate 2
(p. 43)
In plate 2, although the banana flower seems exotic to you, it is ordinary, everyday food to the Philippine native, comparable to our radish! He calls it banana heart and buys it fresh every day in the local market for the equivalent of five cents.

The banana flower, or heart, has been handled like the tulip; the petals have been turned back to form an even more lovely flower, thus using an ordinary food product in a way undreamed of in the Philippine mind. In a lecture-demonstration in Manila one afternoon, I arranged three banana hearts. My Philippine friends were delighted with the result. The moral is clear. Look at your own ordinary life articles with a fresh eye.

The techniques of unusual handling of common materials are the most creative; they are also the most difficult. Knowing that they can be done and knowing that even a small variation is creative, give them a try.

Sensitizing your eyes to beauty is of primary importance. Beauty is all around you just waiting to be recognized. The suggestions for paths to walk in the following chapters can be used by anyone, any time, any place.

PART ONE
Flower Materials

2

What Is Available?

Flowers

How do you start a Character arrangement? Remembering that one criterion for creative flower arranging is unusual or unfamiliar material, what you choose to work with becomes very important. Therefore, the ingredients for Character arrangements will be examined first.

What is available? You can begin with flower blooms with which you are already familiar: varieties of roses, carnations, daffodils, lilies, tulips, daisies, peonies, chrysanthemums, and asters, to mention a few.

When choosing flowers for arrangements, always choose the most perfect, most beautiful, freshest that you can find. However, instead of buying all flowers at the same stage of development, buy one opened flower, one half-opened flower, and one bud. This way, you will have the immediate joy of a beautiful opened flower and the added joy of watching two flowers unfold. Economically, it makes good sense; replacements are stretched over a longer time. Look at it this way too—you are integrating the generations.

What about finding Character elements in flowers? A recent letter from a student, now a bride, gives the answer. After relating her problems in growing perfect, show-type chrysanthemums, she said, "You really begin to appreciate each malformation and how wonderful they are in Ikebana!" Substitute irregularity of pattern for malformation, and you have the answer to how to choose flowers. *Caution*: one irregularity per arrangement is plenty. Perfection is always the best reason for choosing flowers.

Flowers are familiar arranging materials. Where can you find unfamiliar material? Probably right in your own backyard, figuratively speaking.

The largest assortment is in the vast and fascinating field of nature: foliage, seedpods, grasses, driftwood. The rarely explored assortment of abstract and man-made materials is another source. Flowers, foliage, abstracts, and man-mades: these can be combined and recombined in never-ending variations.

Foliage

Foliage are the hardy, long-lived greens of Ikebana. We need to explain their potential because, as a beginner, you may be unaware of it. Their beauties are not as obvious or as spectacular as those of flowers.

Why emphasize a leaf or a branch in preference to flowers in a flower arrangement? Unusualness. Few people think to feature leaves in a flower arrangement. Leaves also can cut down the number of flowers necessary for a pretty arrangement and, therefore, help to cut expenses.

Plate 3
(p. 44) In plate 3 one leaf and a few narcissi equal beauty. The Character element is the handling of the aspidistra leaf, its position and its cut-out shape.

Foliage has numerous unusual characteristics, many of which equal or surpass flowers. Take color for example. We generally think of leaves as green, and most of them are. But there are also highly colored leaves, such as caladiums, begonias, coleus. An outstanding example of color is autumn foliage. Other leaves are variegated in green and white, green and yellow, or other combinations.

Another attribute of greens is high durability. Branches, such as huckleberry, camellia, pine, cedar, and individual leaves, such as cactus and sanseveria, all remain fresh looking for a long, long time when properly conditioned.

Some foliage, when arranged in water, will gradually dry and turn to a soft beige color. Such a dry leaf is usable in dry arrangements later on—an extra bonus. Other leaves will root while in the arrangement, and you can start a new plant. You already know ivy will root.

Leaves have interesting shapes, assorted textures, wonderful fragrance. In order to categorize these assorted attributes for easy reference, a chart has been compiled (p. 196). It's easy to read since each characteristic, with samples, is clearly indicated.

LEAF PLANTS

Foliage for Character arrangements is divided roughly into two classes fashioned after the Japanese Ikebana theory of leaf plants and tree plants.

Leaf plants are those used for the beauty of individual leaves. Even though the leaf plant produces a lovely flower, the leaf is of paramount interest to the Japanese mind. Some examples of leaf plants are iris, hosta, blackberry lily, tulips, and narcissi.

Plates 4, 7 (pp. 45, 48) To illustrate two widely different ways of using leaf plants, examine plates 4 and 7. The arrangement of narcissi keeps this beautiful leaf in its natural, elegant state with no manipulation. The leaves have been arranged in the Peacock pattern which will be discussed later. To use as a centerpiece, cluster narcissi blooms low, in back of the radiating leaves.

The other arrangement, a centerpiece, uses leaves in an opposite manner. Instead of leaving the New Zealand flax in its natural, vertical condition, a ribbonlike effect has been created, a feeling of summer rain.

To get the effect, use your thumbnail. Starting at the central rib, rip the leaf beyond its outer edge. Be careful of your fingers; some leaves are sharp. After the first ribbon, make another half an inch or so farther up the rib.

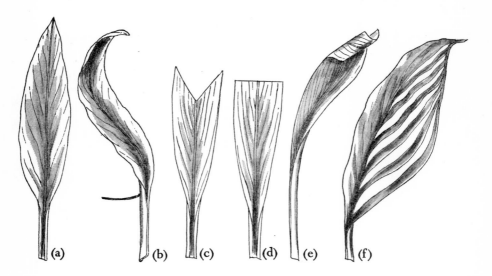

FIG. 1. Shaping broad-blade leaves: (a) natural ti leaf; (b) curved by wire and tape along back rib; wire cut at stem end; (c) wedge shaped; (d) sliced; (e) gently furled; (f) shredded.

Make the ribbons as wide or as narrow as you think best.

To vary the effect, stop your thumb at the selvage edge of the leaf. Stopping short gives a looped effect, such as is shown in figure 1(f). You can "loop" one side of an aspidistra leaf, both sides, or even half a leaf.

Certain leaves can be curved, bent, trimmed, or knotted into different shapes (figs. 1, 2). They can be edged with pinking scissors, scalloped, wired, or reduced in size. How to wire is shown in the chapter on equipment (p. 126).

The aspidistra leaf is common; its counterpart in Hawaii is the *ti* (pronounced "tee"), and plants of both are used extensively to decorate public places because they are so durable. Finding leaves to use is a matter of looking around.

If you live in a temperate zone, no one should object to your cutting new shoots of the plentiful, common plant, skunk cabbage, in early spring. At this stage of its growth it has no odor. Search for it in damp places in the woods. The

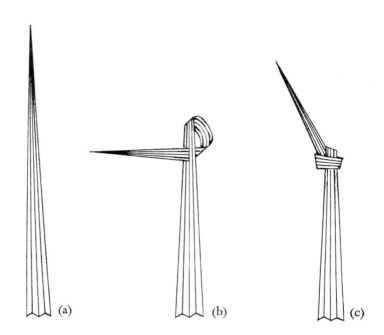

Fig. 2. Shaping narrow-blade leaves: (a) natural lauhala leaf; (b) tip of leaf pushed through small slit; (c) bow-knot.

pointed purplish leaves would be effective with two pink carnations or clustered grapes.

Don't overlook an easy source for leaves, a garden. Grow onions, parsley, chives. The rhubarb plant is a real beauty with bright red stalks and veined leaves. Swiss chard is attractive. Rhubarb-chard has gorgeous purple and bronze convoluted leaves.

The cabbage family offers flowering kale, which is used frequently in Japan during New Year festivities. Crinkly Chinese cabbage is used in Ikebana also. Carrot and beet tops make good greenery.

Vegetable counters of specialty stores should carry fresh red lettuce, curly endive, and escarole. These vegetable greens are not ordinarily longlasting in an arrangement but they can fill in during an emergency. They are always usable afterwards in stews.

Tree Plants

Tree plants are used in Ikebana for their beautiful, unusual branching qualities and unusual characteristics of line or mass. Tree plants include bushes and shrubs as well as trees.

Since branches from tree plants are basic Ikebana materials, Japanese florists carry large supplies. Growing and distributing flower materials is big business.

For you, getting greens may be a problem. Check these possibilities. You might search in country areas where you may cut a branch or two without breaking conservation laws. Never take more than you need. Your city botanical garden may help you. Watch, also, for the city tree-trimming schedule when your city or county frees telephone wires from exuberant growth.

Another possibility may be discarded trimmings from private gardens of friends. It is possible that commercial nurseries or greenhouses can help you, especially if you are a customer. When you order flowers, florists normally include some greens. Always ask.

The best solution is to grow your own greens. Suggest to your friends that housewarming gifts or first-year anniversary gifts of potted plants would be the most welcome gift selection.

The plants listed below have been roughly divided into two categories of leaf and tree plants. More detailed information on colors and special characteristics can be found in the Plant Identification section (p. 200).

Check with the best nurseryman in town for suggestions on what you can grow easily as a beginner. Tell him you want plants to use for flower arranging; they must have durable leaves when cut.

The plants below will live well either in pots or in the ground for a considerable time with proper feeding and attention. Always buy the largest plant you can afford; one large plant is better than two small ones.

artemisia albula

asparagus family

aspidistra family

begonias

dusty meadow rue

flax, New Zealand

hosta, or funkia

hydrangea

lily family

pandanus, or lauhala

papyrus

peperomia

nandina

Solomon's seal

ti family

TREE PLANTS WITH ATTRACTIVE BRANCHING

azalea

buttonwood

carissa

cotoneaster (horizontalis)

cryptomeria (cedar)

daphne

eucalyptus family

euonymus

fig family

hardy orange

hawthorne

Japanese yew

mock orange

osmanthus

pine family

pittosporum

privet

pyracantha

red castorbean

spice bush

Sweet Bay magnolia

Dry Materials: Seedpods, Grasses, Driftwood

In frosty winter, fresh flower materials are not readily available except at high cost. With a bit of forethought you can still take advantage of nature's offerings. Enterprising flower arrangers can always have "money in the bank," so to speak.

Think ahead. During summer and fall, varieties of grasses and seedpods are ripe for drying. Autumn usually offers the best selection, but summer has the iris seedpod, tulip pods, cattails, and so on.

What you collect and when you collect it depends on where you live; that is, temperate zone, tropics, desert.

For example, cattails are ready for drying in early June in the Philippines; in Japan, cattails are ready in July; in the mid-west United States, August or September.

Natural drying is no problem. Simply tie stems of your material together and hang the group upside down from a ceiling hook in a dry place. Cover with newspaper at the top and leave the bottom open. Dampness and moisture remaining in the plant cause rot and mildew. Dust is also detrimental to beauty! Eliminate these two nuisances by hanging in a dry place and covering with paper, and you'll have pretty dry material.

With the emphasis on ecology and conservation laws, you must be careful what you cut. Many states, fortunately, have strict laws. It is forbidden to take plant life from state or national parks, roadside picnic areas, camping grounds, and other spots. Always check before your outing. A telephone call to your local forestry or agriculture center will help to guide you.

If permitted, there are many weeds to gather; they look fantastic in arrangements. As James Russell Lowell in his *Fable for Critics* said, "A weed is no more than a flower in disguise!" Collect some.

The mullein possibly may not fall under conservation laws. Mullein can grow straight and tall, or it can assume contorted shapes. Two or three stalks around 20 inches high are plenty for a nice arrangement. Use them natural, or spray-paint them black; use with brilliant gladioli for a modern contrast. Keep gladioli short enough to show off the mullein. Perhaps the tallest should be about 14 inches high.

Good for several weeks is the colorful sumac with its pointed, dark-red clusters. Use in a tall, narrow-necked jar, cutting the sumac quite long. Sumac has interestingly jointed branches; therefore, study the bush carefully before you cut to insure getting a shaped branch that will fit a spot in your home.

Other "weeds" to consider are the bristly star thistle,

milkweed pods, and dock. Dock is an attractive, reddish-brown, small-berried plant. Look also for teasels, which come in oval and round shapes, all thorny; grasses, such as the bunny tails, tumbleweed, rust-brown buckwheat; wheat heads either in a green or dry stage. Unripe barley is interesting.

Others that you should not overlook are poppyseed capsules and woodroses. Okra is attractive bleached white. Thistle sage, lipstick pods, and the fruiting stalks of Kaffir corn are beautiful.

Driftwood hunting has become almost a national pastime, so driftwood in many areas is a scarce item. However, tree branches, dried, can be used, as well as roots. Don't limit driftwood hunting to the sea shore; also look in the mountains, near lakes, and in swampy places.

Japanese always handle dry branches, roots, twigs, and driftwood with as much joy and respect as they do flower blooms. A "dead" branch is not dead to them, but only in a cycle of the life pattern. Arranging it indicates recognition and respect for the large pattern of nature.

A gnarled branch can give strength, age, and dignity to an arrangement. Try it. When you understand this bit of Japanese philosophy, using "dead" branches becomes more meaningful.

The above suggestions will offer ripe hunting grounds, but nature has still more to give. Consider treasures from the seas and the ocean and treasures from the ground such as rocks, pebbles, stones, and sand.

Abstract and Man-made Materials

There is little question that nature provides the best source of materials for Character arrangement, but let's not overlook products from our modern world.

If natural materials are difficult to find, remember you are a product of today's age, visual-minded. Observe closely the daily life around you. Growing up with television, slick magazines, pop art, films, and photography, you are acutely aware of bold designs, color, shininess, and man-made objects. Look for materials to emphasize these aspects of life in your arrangements. I have used colored communication-wiring successfully, for instance. Flower arranging must live in today's world.

The common, ordinary household scouring pad fired my imagination. Copper- and brass-mesh pads have been used in dozens of arrangements, and I selected two for this bride's book, plates 9 and 31. Plate 9 is designed to be placed on a tray for a TV dinner. Bunny tails and a few straw flowers are arranged in a diagonal pattern. Compare the use of the mesh pad in these two photographs.

Plates 9, 31 (pp. 50, 158)

Although you can use the circular copper scouring pad as it comes from the grocery store, please note that the one in the picture is in a rectangular shape. Unravel the pad by unclipping the metal fastener, then reroll it in the form you want. Here, the edges are tucked into the pad, and the unit holds the arrangement firmly.

You can keep a fresh scouring pad and a small assortment of colorful straw flowers in your silverware drawer. When necessary, make the arrangement in a few minutes, matching whatever tray accessories you plan.

As a beginner without preconceived ideas, perhaps you may find interest in vinyl-covered wire or man-made Styrofoam balls on flexible stems. (See plate 21.) Such materials give an ordinary arrangement rhythm, movement, and interest, and highlight a conversation-arousing piece. Surely these aims are worthy.

Plate 21 (p. 149)

If you are one who is cautious about abstract materials, yet you wish to experiment, use only materials that have an intrinsic beauty to your mind's eye. Peacock feathers have intrinsic beauty in most eyes, and in mine in particular. Only two are used in plate 6, but with stunning effect.

Plate 6 (p. 47)

The following list should serve as a springboard. Each material has been chosen for its individual attraction for me. See if there is one that appeals to you:

candles

copper wire: thin, but stiff enough to be self-supporting

copper sheeting

cork

wired tinsel cord in gold or silver

feathers

feather dusters: red color

kitchen scouring pads

plastic rain

plastic straws

screening in copper or brass

small colored beads on flexible stems

stiffened rope: use heavy starch, medium-weight rope (try in collages)

Styrofoam balls: decorated in flocked velvet, in frosted glaze, or undecorated

Styrofoam blocks

vinyl-covered wire: all colors (takes spray paint beautifully)

You will find many of these materials at florist supply houses or import-export stores. Look in the yellow pages of your telephone book, then go to the shop and browse. One look is worth a hundred descriptions.

3

Why Choose a Particular Piece?

With a repertoire of materials to choose from, let's examine the answer to the question, "Why choose a particular piece of flower material over the others?" Because you value its artistic and physical characteristics! In this answer lies the secret of creative flower arrangement. Does that sound too simple? In simplicity lies beauty.

Artistic Characteristics

COLOR

The artistic characteristics of flower material are color, texture, and shape. Color is the most obvious. The visual impact of color for the creative flower arranger is very strong; sometimes so strong that it's the only artistic element used in combining materials.

Traditionally, the primary colors are red, yellow, and blue. Traditional color combinations are monochromatic (tints and shades of one color); analogous (adjacent colors on chart); and contrasting (opposites). Young people have joyfully exploded many color theories with beautiful results in home decor. They have thoroughly explored the color field. But has this exploration included flower arranging?

The color diagram used for Character arranging (fig. 3) has four primary colors. Certainly in flower arranging we must consider green as a basic color. As you are well aware,

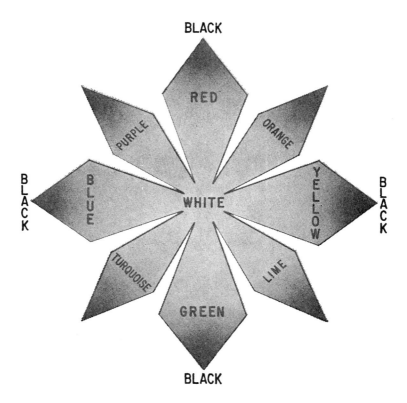

Fɪɢ. 3. Color diagram. Traditional color combinations are: monochromatic, one color ranging from white to black; analogous, adjacent colors; contrasting, opposite colors.

each color can be muted infinitely; the chart of eight colors is merely to set you thinking.

For first efforts with a Character color arrangement, work with a monochromatic scheme, using shades of green leaves and green plastic balls. Some of my favorite arrangements, on the other hand, use near-contrast colors.

To your present color knowledge let me add the classical Ikebana way with color.

Classical Ikebana bases color combinations on the ratio of colors in nature. Imagine you are on a hill, contemplating the horizon with forest, desert, or ocean in between.

At a distance, the view appears to be one general color—say, green for a forest; there may be the sparkle of a river or a color splash from a flowering tree.

Get in the car, drive to such an area, get out of the car, and look. You will find that the forest is not a uniform green, but infinite shadings of green. You will also find other colors—brown, gray, blue, black, beige—in tree bark, stones, the earth, insects. Although green predominates, the other colors are there. Always, too, there is a brilliant flower, a patch of berries, or something vivid. Often there is a special element, such as a singing bird.

The same revelation would hold true for the ocean or the desert. The most rewarding value of nature is that she never demands our attention, but if we give it we see the infinite variety present, not only in color, but in patterns and textures as well.

Japan, as a temperate-zone country, is predominately green. An Ikebana uses foliage with splashes of color and usually one accent value, like a grace note. The "grace note" is present in every creative Ikebana.

The emotional impact of a classical Ikebana is one of quiet serenity; of a forest path, or a green, green garden. The quiet greens always outweigh the color volume of the flowers. Ikebana, in total, adds up to high livability in a home. It gives the viewer a feeling of a breath of fresh air or a walk in the country which couldn't be taken on a rainy day.

TEXTURE

A second artistic characteristic of flower material is texture. Texture describes the surface structure, the covering "skin" of an object. We react to textures emotionally through sight and touch. Many people find the urge to touch something new or unfamiliar almost irresistible.

Textures can be appealing, as in the velvety petals of roses; intriguing, like the veined pattern in wet Petosky

PLATE 2. Chinese bell flowers, bird's-nest fern leaves, small red grapes, and a banana flower on a board. Small bunches of new bananas appear at the base of the banana flower.

PLATE 3. A cut-out aspidistra leaf with three narcissi in a hanging bamboo container, an example of minimal flower material.

PLATE 4. Narcissus flowers and leaves with pine in a brown-and-gold-speckled lacquer container.

PLATE 5. Philippine woodroses, ocean coral, and dry seedpods in a "porthole" container.

PLATE 6. Peacock feathers with massed baby's breath in a blue Italian hand-blown glass vase. No holder; only thin wire keeps baby's breath together.

PLATE 7. Split New Zealand flax leaves and orange-red star lilies in a yellow glass boat.

PLATE 8. Sea fan with glossy anthurium in a glass container. The shine of the glass harmonizes with the brilliance of the anthurium texture. Center sea fan is 14 inches wide, an indication of the depth perspective.

PLATE 9. Bunny tails and straw flowers anchored in a refolded kitchen scouring pad in a slanting pattern. Wooden container turned upside down acts as background.

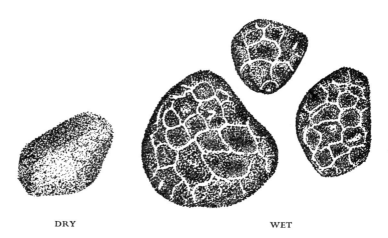

FIG. 4. Wet Petosky stones showing detailed veining.

stones (fig. 4), or the shininess of the anthurium flower;
beautiful, in a creamy calla lily; deceiving in the cardone
puffs which look soft but are actually spiny, or sea fans
which look so lacy and fragile, yet are very tough. Textures
can be distasteful (to me), like that of the pitcher plant
with its hairy throat.

Textures lend continuing interest to flower arrangements
so you should try to make sure that viewers become aware
of them. It's true that texture awareness seldom happens
quickly because viewers normally react first to color. Varying textures in an arrangement adds appreciably to its
aesthetic interest.

Plate 8 The black-and-white photograph (plate 8) emphasizes the
(p. 49) airiness of the sea fan. You must look closely to see its
spongy covering on the skeletal ribs which once were the
animal. There is a strong contrast of textures in combining
the sea fan with the glossy anthurium, a rather unusual one.
Frequently sea fan is arranged with bird of paradise, whose
texture is in harmony.

You may need a little help at first in combining textures;
therefore, an analysis has been included in the chart titled
Relating Flower Material to Container (p. 198).

SHAPE

Shape, technically, is a physical characteristic, but since the special shape of any particular piece of flower material may give the arrangement its artistic emphasis, shape must come under the artistic category.

Each piece of flower material grown by nature has small differences, even within its own species. To be specific, a quirk of growth could be as follows: an unusually thick needle growth; a unique shape of a leaf, fresh or dry; an unusual petal formation; a mutation of color in a common flower; an abrupt angle to a branch. Any of these can put ordinary material on a special level, immediately raising its artistic value. Although such "quirks" may sound uncommon, actually they are not. The trick is to recognize the treasure. To do this, take a closer look at the flower.

During the early learning process, right now if at all possible, take the time to learn how to examine or "read" the form of any piece of flower material. Let the flowers "talk" to you, ridiculous as this sounds. If you acquire the knack of studying a flower for shape and texture values, without being overwhelmed by its color value, you are well on the road to aesthetic, creative flower arranging.

For guidance, ask yourself some pertinent questions while examining a flower. Is the stem curved, even a little bit? Which is the back and which is the front of the flower, stem, and bloom? Is the head ball-shaped, flat, heart-shaped? Is it thick or thin? Are there many petals or only a few? Are the petals single or double? Is the flower bloom composed of flowerets? a single spathe? spikes? Are the edges serrated, lobed, smooth?

Noticing natural details puts a beginner in the frame of mind to take full advantage of any particular distinction.

Here's an example. An aspect of arranging that is consistently overlooked by beginners is the "set" of a flower face. The set of the flower face is important to graceful, beautiful arranging. Reference is made here not to the surface quality of flowers or to their general shape, but to the specific angle at which any flower looks best to a viewer. It is not merely a haphazard angle.

If you are skeptical, try this. Revolve any flower stem slowly in your fingers while studying the face. You will find a point at which the flower looks at you. Arrange it in the vase with the face looking up at you.

Flowers can also be arranged looking at each other, a favorite way with many Ikebana schools. Whichever way you choose, maintain harmony and grace by keeping all flowers either on "talking terms" with each other or on "talking terms" with you.

Physical Characteristics

SIZE

The size of any piece of material in relation to the others controls proportion in the arrangement. Size can also dictate its position. Be careful, for example, of too-large blossoms in relation to too-small branches. Be guided by their proportions in nature. If you are not sure when planning combinations of materials, check in the library. Mainly, your visual sense should tell you what is especially pleasing.

Flower blooms come in a wide variety of sizes, even in individual species such as the chrysanthemum which has the large football mums as well as the delicate pompoms.

Greens also come in varied sizes. The chart on Attributes of Fresh Leaves (p. 196) will give you many samples from unusually small to unusually large.

FRAGRANCE

Fragrance, like color, gives another sensual dimension to flower arranging. Of the many choices available, consider these: pungent eucalyptus (hundreds of varieties); the astringent odor of water lilies; the strong but pleasant daphne; the elusive scent of cymbidium orchid sprays; the haunting osmanthus; the spicy yew; the subtle fragrance of citrus leaves; the fresh smell of bruised surinam cherry leaves.

Each locale has its speciality. Certainly you have already thought of your favorite, which may be roses or carnations. Leafy fragrances were emphasized to expand your knowledge. Your nurseryman is invaluable here.

A word of caution on fragrance: some people are allergic to strong scents. Therefore, particularly for centerpieces, use care in choosing. Elusive, subtle perfumes are better than heavy, overpowering scents.

Too much fragrance or too many conflicting fragrances give people an overcrowded feeling. Be discreet in your choice. Scents that suggest spaciousness and the great outdoors are pine, citrus, fresh herbs, and familiar flower smells: lily of the valley, carnation, and violet.

If you desire a special scent for a dinner party and the centerpiece is non-scented, tape a scented sachet or fragrance tablet to the inside leg of the dining table.

GROWTH PATTERNS

A specific growth characteristic of living materials is that each has a front and a back. In most materials this is obvious; no one can mistake the front and the back of a magnolia leaf, for example.

However, recognizing the front and back of some plant materials, notably evergreens, is difficult. This is why you were asked to rotate the flower stem. It showed you how to find the angle at which the flower grew in nature, with the front facing the sun.

Most beginning flower arrangers ignore the fact that pine, cedar, spruces, and members of the asparagus family all have a front and a back. They look identical all the way around. Cedar branches are often arranged with the reverse side, rather than the front of the material, on view.

The secret of recognizing the front from the back of these needlelike materials is the growth pattern of the needles. They grow toward the light and sun; therefore, the north side, or underside, of a branch will have few, if any, needles. When arranging these materials, check first, then arrange them face up.

Another growth characteristic is the fact that all tips of branches (both trees and shrubs) turn up. Only the weeping willow has tips that hang down. Observe this phenomenon for yourself by checking any shrub or tree.

Therefore, when arranging branches, remember to keep tips pointing up, especially when filling in stems around the rim of the container in a centerpiece. This simple trick will give an added vitality to any arrangement.

In this same line of thought, to give vibrancy to your flower arrangements, be sure that each stem of material clears the rim of the vase. Arrangements where flower stems relax on the container rim lose an "alive" feeling.

When studying the growth pattern of trees and bushes, you will note that some branches grow to the right of the trunk and some to the left. This knowledge can be used advantageously. If a vase is to be placed in a right-hand corner of a room, a branch is needed that "faces" in the proper direction, not one that looks into the wall. However, if the branch is the only one you have, and it doesn't fit the space, perhaps you can twist it gently to conform. (See Manual Techniques, p. 58.)

SILHOUETTE

The silhouette of any flower material can give clues to arranging it. Vertical materials, such as bulrushes, equisetum, cattails, bunny tails, rushes, milkweed pods, and long-needled pine, all look well standing tall in their natural fashion.

Feathery materials, such as acacia, baby's breath, types of statice, split leaves of New Zealand flax, the phoenix palm, and spiraea, all look well in cascading styles to accentuate their gracefulness.

On the other hand, emphasizing the exact opposite of the natural silhouette makes for creative flower arranging.

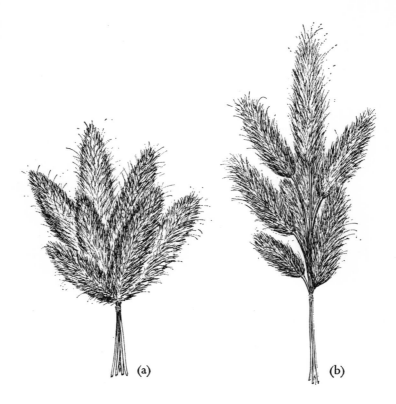

FIG. 5. Bunny tails clustered with wire holding stems: (a) in massed effect; (b) in line effect.

Use bunny tails clustered instead of individually placed. Cluster five to seven tails to each group for easy handling. Figures 5(a) and (b) show you two ways to bunch them for two different effects. Try them with branches of fall foliage to replace flowers.

The cattails bent into an angular pattern in the photograph on page 96 are quite the opposite of their original growing style. The effect is eye-catching. Every material has a natural silhouette and a potential for an opposite. Angled bulrushes are very popular in Japanese arrangements. Perhaps you can think of an interesting way to place them.

DURABILITY

Fundamental to any beautiful, fresh flower arrangement is its lasting freshness. An arrangement that droops an hour after its creation is a disappointment indeed.

What plant characteristics are to be observed when choosing materials for long-lasting arrangements? In botanical language, fleshy plants, or those with leathery, heavy leaves have longer-lasting qualities. Transpiration, or losing water through leaves and stems, is slower with fleshy plants.

Good examples of long-lasting leaves are those of the cactus family, rubber tree, camellia, sanseveria, and the monstera.

Thin leaves lose water rapidly and thus wilt quickly. To prevent transpiration in an emergency, try spreading white vaseline on thin-skinned leaves. White vaseline seals off the pores. This is a suggestion you might wish to use if you are making an arrangement for public display.

Some rather fragile-looking plants are durable. The feathery artemisia is one, and so are some species of baby's breath. In fact, the gypsophila makes beautiful preserved material. Don't throw it away; hang it up to dry and use it with roses, spray-painting it the same color as the flowers.

To keep flowers and leaves longer, proper conditioning is essential. In fact, it is so essential that a complete chapter has been devoted to conditioning and preserving.

4

Manual Techniques

One evening in Washington, D.C., a noted Japanese Ikebana master began his flower-arranging demonstration by picking up a large group of beautiful flower materials. In one movement he stashed them into a tall vase and announced, "International style!" The audience laughed, because such is the impression many Western flower arrangements give.

The Ikebana master then removed the group, selected one branch and two flowers, and with a few deft movements of his fingers created a breathtaking Ikebana.

The "few deft movements of his fingers" are the important words. You can educate your fingers to curve flower material just as you can educate your eye to detect interesting quirks in materials. Anyone can learn the mechanics for making flower materials stay in place.

Curving

Training your fingers to handle branches and leaves skillfully is fun. It's fun to change a straight branch into one with rhythmic curves. Many types of foliage, both leaf and tree plants, have the capability of being curved.

The mechanics of bending take two or three times' practice, but they are not difficult (fig. 6). You will soon learn to recognize how much pressure to apply, how to get

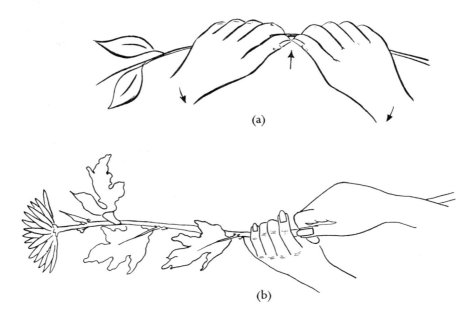

FIG. 6. Hand positions for bending: (a) branches; (b) flower stems (twist and bend).

the skin of a branch barely to crack, how to achieve the half-break, and, most important, when to stop!

(1) Use both hands on the branch. Both hands warm the area and give better control than finger tips alone.
(2) Keep the branch close to your heart, not at arm's length. Concentrate.
(3) Exert downward pressure with the thumbs guiding.
(4) Move hands up and down the branch, keeping pressure even. Never bend continuously and heavily in one place.
(5) For a double curve, bend the lower part of the branch downward, then reverse the branch to the straight area and bend again, downward.

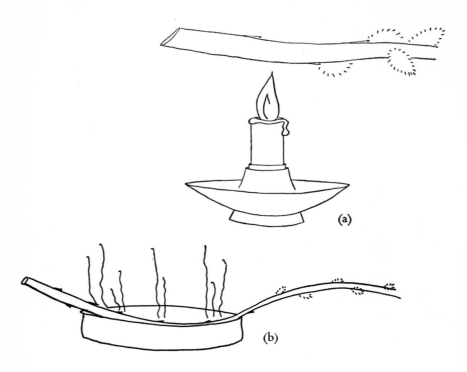

FIG. 7. Bending branches using (a) flame, and (b) boiling water.

Most people tend to exert a more even pressure downward, which is the reason I suggest it. Bend upward if it's easier for you.

A candle flame or boiling water can also be used to make bending easier, as shown in figures 7(a), (b). Work quickly, bend the branch, wire it in place. Keep the branch in cool water for several hours after either of these treatments. Steam from a tea kettle is also effective in warming branches.

Never trust to luck that the branch will turn out all right. Always plan, before you bend, exactly how you wish the greens to look.

Test by placing the straight branch in your container and putting the container where the arrangement is to be dis-

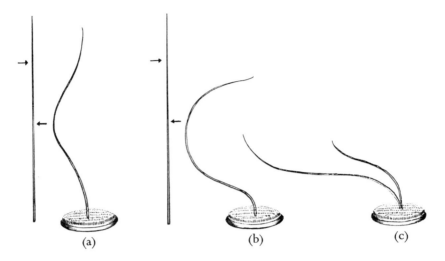

Fig. 8. Models for bending: (a) vertical; (b) curved; (c) vertical branch in horizontal position, with a coordinated second branch.

played. Gently force the branch into the curve you think you want after gauging the amount of curve you'll need.

While it is in place, check the visual balance of the branch both to the container and to the setting. Remember, curved branches occupy less linear space than straight ones. Be sure you have the proper length, including the curve, before bending the branch.

If the branch is heavier than your little finger, use one of the methods indicated below to warm and soften it prior to bending.

To teach bending methods, Japanese teachers use a model and insist on exact duplication of all curves and spaces between curves. Such a method teaches coordination of eye and hand. Sometimes it's easy to imagine how you want the branch to look, but executing the pattern needs finger and mind coordination. To help you visualize some attractive curves, three simple patterns for the dominating branch of an arrangement are sketched (figs. 8a–c).

Many tree and leaf plants are capable of being curved, but not all. How can you tell? Without some experience, testing a branch is the only way. Use a small branch for testing.

The following plants, commonly available, can all be curved:

EVERGREENS	WILLOWS
arborvitae	corkscrew willow
asparagus family	dragon willow
cedar	fasciated willow (fantail)
cypress	pussy willow
juniper	weeping willow
pine	silver willow

ORNAMENTAL PLANTS

apricot	honeysuckle
bulrushes	huckleberry
camellia	lemon myrtle
cycad palm	mock orange
daphne	osage orange
euonymous	privet
flowering cherry	scotch broom
flowering peach	spiraea

Since you are a newcomer to flower arranging, you may not know that some materials—the bulrush and the cycad palm, for example— need preliminary drying before curving. When freshly cut, these materials are brittle and snap in half if bending is tried.

Leave them out of water from one to three days. You can tell when they are pliable by testing gently. The cycad fronds should be laid flat and weighted to prevent curling while drying. I put them on a floor and cover them with newspapers weighted with magazines. Be sure all frond tips are flat, not out of line. Palms are hardy, sometimes taking several days to become pliable enough to bend.

A trick for curving cycads nicely is to dampen them and

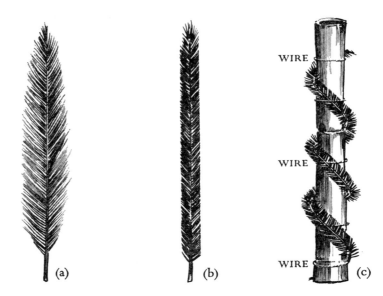

FIG. 9. Stages in curving flower material: (a) natural cycad palm frond; (b) trimmed; (c) damp frond wrapped and wired around bamboo.

wrap them around a 3-inch-diameter pole after the preliminary drying. Usually trim the fronds short because they are very prickly to handle. Then, curve them around the pole widely, as in figure 9. Wire them in place and dry for several days or a few weeks, depending on your climate. Use them in their natural beige color, or coat them with spray paint.

All references so far have been to curving foliage, but flower stems can also be curved. They are more fragile. Massaging the stems warms the cells and makes bending easier. After massaging gently, make your hands flow over the stem area and exert pressure in the downward motion.

When manipulating any live material, do everything as quickly and lightly as possible, much as when handling pie crust dough. Keep the flowers from getting worn out before they reach your arrangement.

Woody stems, such as chrysanthemum stems, should be twisted as you bend. The outer stem is so crisp that it will snap under ordinary bending, but with the simultaneous twist-bend method you can curve them. Check internal wiring techniques too.

Much of the charm of Ikebana is achieved through the use of curved materials. Arrangements are never static. As you read further in the book, you will discover that you can go one more step beyond the bending described above. You can curve a branch to achieve a three-dimensional look.

Sculpturing

Much foliage has another special capability: angles and spaces may be sculptured from it. The word "sculptured" is used advisedly in this study of Character arrangements.

Historically, sculpturing is an art of subtraction. An artist chipped away pieces from his chosen block of marble, wood, or other material until an image emerged. Modern sculptors often use the addition of materials to create the image. Today's art museums exhibit infinite nuances of modern sculpture involving materials of plastic, wood, metals, glass—all added to themselves or to each other.

Ikebana encompasses both types of sculpturing: subtraction and addition. Avant-garde Ikebana uses the addition of materials, particularly evident in exhibition creations (some over 40 feet in height). Pieces of egg shell, bamboo, copper, bits of glass mirrors, metals, or any other feasible material are fastened over preshaped pieces of driftwood, plywood, cardboard, etc. Most Ikebana teachers and many students experiment with this type of addition-sculpture.

Classical Ikebana uses the technique of subtraction. This skill is easy when you know what to look for. Beautiful, unexpected forms can be "discovered" in a branch by simply trimming away excess twigs, excess branches, interfering leaves. Being able to see these lines and spaces in flower material is a rewarding personal experience because it's your own discovery.

How can you judge an adequate branch? Experience sharpens the eye, but the magic key is this: Check the growth pattern of the branches. Do the small branches alternate on a mainstem? fan out? grow parallel? grow in an intricate mass? The maple has particularly lovely branch-

Plate 11 (p. 92)

ing characteristics. In plate 11, drastic subtraction has taken place, leaving only a few special branches.

As you have already surmised, twigs that grow far apart give you little chance to make angles or spaces. Obviously, one long, straight branch will have little of interest to sculpt. If you are a gardener, look for woody plants. They tend to have better branching characteristics than herbaceous plants.

Particular materials do lend themselves ordinarily to sculpting techniques. Most of the following materials cannot be curved owing to a characteristic brittleness inherent in their growth, which means they'll break if you try to curve them. But they can be cut and shaped, since the branching qualities frequently are interesting.

CHOICE MATERIALS FOR SCULPTURING

azalea	nandina
crabapple	old pine
dried woodrose vines	old croton bushes
eucalyptus family	osage orange
hawthorne	pear (old, gnarled branches)
holly	plum
loquat	pomegranate
magnolia	pyracantha
maple	quince
mulberry	zigzag plant

Experience has shown that the most interesting branches to sculpt are often found in the lower portions of a shrub. Novices in cutting tend to look for interesting lines at the top of a branch which sometimes feathers out to a point. Older growth provides more gnarled twistings, more character emphasis.

We have been discussing sculpturing space from large branches, but do not overlook the importance of small areas even with individual stems of roses, mums, peonies, and other flowers with profuse leaves.

True art comes only when the artist knows what to leave out, so trim drastically. Remember that elimination of leaves and buds not only improves the use of space in your arrangement, it also acts to preserve the flower blooms longer.

Stabilizing

Anchoring flower material firmly on a needlepoint holder, or *kenzan* in Japanese, may seem like "no big thing." It is, though, if the arrangement falls over. For stabilizing purposes, divide stems into the lightweight and the heavyweight. Two simple techniques answer the problem for lightweight stems.

One: Cut the stem straight across. Do not cut it on the slant, despite previous hints you may have read to the contrary for water absorption. Proper conditioning will take care of water absorption; most important is to have your stem firmly placed. As large a base area on the stem as possible is needed for a stable arrangement, and a straight-cut stem gives more contact surface than a slanted tip.

Two: Grasp the stem firmly with both hands. Keeping it upright, push the stem well down on the needlepoints until the stem hits bottom. Then, still holding firmly down, slant the stem to the desired angle. Thus the needles catch both the end and the sides of the stem for better anchoring.

A heavyweight branch could measure from the thickness of your little finger on up. Cut heavyweight branch-ends at a mild slant for easier insertion into the *kenzan*. Counterbalance with two smaller branches on the needlepoints, keep-

FIG. 10. Top view of stem placement in a kenzan.

ing all three branches away from the *kenzan*'s perimeter. Place them as indicated in the sketch (fig. 10).

Sometimes even with good positioning on the *kenzan* a branch may be difficult to balance. Eight suggestions are listed below; one of them should solve your engineering problem.

(1) Eliminate weight along the branch by cutting off excess leaves, berries, or fruit.

Plate 12
(p. 93)

(Example: In plate 12, maple branches were reduced to $\frac{1}{3}$ of their original heavy foliage. Perfect balance is easier in the narrow opening of the Japanese classical-style old lacquered gourd.)

(2) Reduce the number of seedpods or flowers.

(3) Reduce the size of clustered flowers, fruit, or pods.

(4) Cut the branch shorter.

(5) Dry out the material in a low oven (110 degrees), if possible.

(6) Change the torque of the branch by twisting gently in the opposite direction.

(7) If a branch tip persists in "looking the wrong way," use fingers to twist the stem gently to the proper facing. (Example: In plate 12 the new maple tip in the front had to be twisted to the proper angle.)

(8) If all else fails, wire the branch to a heavier stem. The extra stem will give needed contact surface to anchor in the *kenzan*.

Manual Techniques 67

So much for light- and heavy-weight stems. What about the arrangement as a whole? How can you steady it? If you know about floral clay, that's the best answer for beginners. Specific, never-fail instructions for claying in the *kenzan* are given under the Equipment chapter.

With an Ikebana instructor, you might also be taught balance through using an extra *kenzan* for counterbalance. (See sun-moon *kenzan* under Equipment, p. 119.)

Anchoring

Flowers and individual leaves have different problems of anchoring than branches. Many flowers, especially those used for centerpieces, have slender stems: carnations, roses, ranunculus, daisies, etc. A variety of ways to anchor them immovably on a *kenzan* is suggested below.

(1) Wrap the stem in small squares of tissue paper (fig. 11).
(2) Push the thin stem into a larger, more porous stalk, such as a calla lily stem (fig. 12).
(3) Put the stem into a clear plastic drinking straw (fig. 13).
(4) Wrap the stem with matching floral tape (fig. 14).
(5) Fold an inch of the bottom stem of leaves up to give greater contact area (fig. 15).
(6) Accordion-pleat the bottom edge of the leaf for extra bulk (fig. 16).
(7) Wire the stem to a small stick for support. Use two thin wires, one at the top, one at the bottom; or spiral a wire all along the length of the support stick (fig. 17).
(8) Use a heavy wire, or a stick such as a skewer, and insert it inside the hollow-stemmed flowers. Examples: amaryllis, water lily, daffodil (fig. 18).

Some flowers, even though they are not actually hollow inside, can have a wire pushed carefully through the stem for extra support and for curving the stem.

The heavy professional wire used in internal wiring is

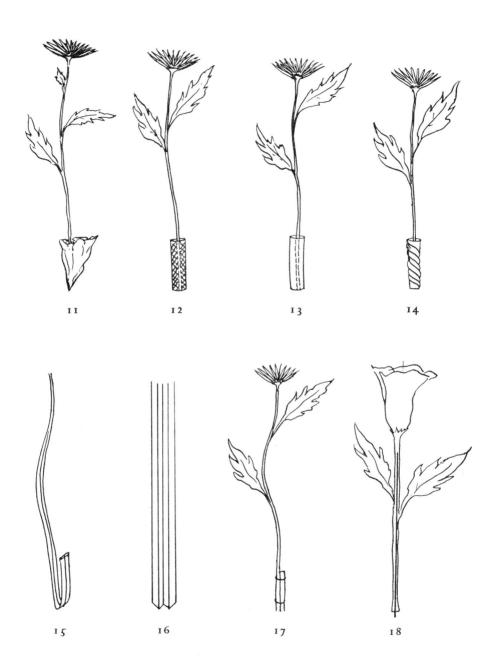

11 12 13 14

15 16 17 18

FIG. 11–18. Anchoring methods for thin-stemmed flowers or leaves.

No. 18. The advantage of internal wiring scarcely needs to be pointed out. All the mechanics are hidden so neatly —a highly desirable factor, particularly with centerpieces, always subject to close scrutiny.

(1) Cut the flower to the desired length.
(2) Cut the wire three inches longer.
(3) Insert the wire into the stalk, guiding carefully so that the wire won't come out any place along the stem.
(4) Push the wire clear through the entire stem until you can see it in the flower. Pull it back slightly to hide it.
(5) Trim off the extra wire.
(6) Bend the wired stem to fit the arrangement design.
(7) Make sure water in the container is high.

Not all flowers or leaves will accept internal wiring. Of those that do accept it, some are easier to wire than others. Daffodils are very easy. Calla lilies are more difficult. Narcissi are easy.

Below are flowers and leaves that have been tested. They can be wired internally.

FLOWERS		LEAVES
amaryllis	lotus	clivia
asters	poinsettias	irises
bachelor's buttons	shasta daisies	gladioli
calla lilies	sweet william	narcissus leaves
chrysanthemums	tulips	
daffodils	waterlilies	
gerbera daisies		

For amaryllis and waterlilies, use either wire or a slender stick. Some varieties of chrysanthemums will take wiring, and some will not. Generally speaking, leaves with ribs cannot be wired internally but they can be wired externally. External wiring is naturally faster, but take care that your cellophane tape and wire aren't visible after arranging.

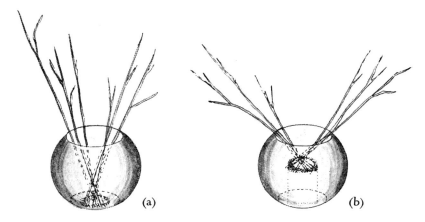

FIG. 19. Kenzan in bowls: (a) too deep; (b) properly raised.

(1) Lay medium-weight wire no. 22 along the length of the back rib.
(2) Tape the wire carefully with one piece of tape. Wire must run the full length from tip to stem.
(3) Curve the leaf.

Try external wiring with aspidistra leaves or rubber tree, magnolia, or *ti* leaves, or New Zealand flax. Until you learn to curve iris leaves with your fingers, wire will be a great help to you.

Small Problems

Many small problems in mechanics plague the beginner. Often they can be solved with a little know-how.

Arranging many flowers "international style," in deep crystal or silver containers, Paul Revere-style bowls, or deep salad bowls is easy. Using just a few flowers is difficult. When stuck in needlepoint holders, the flowers often seem peculiarly stiff and ungraceful, as in figure 19(a).

The solution? Raise the needlepoint holder (fig. 19b).

Then you will find that the flowers slant gracefully, and no one at dinner has to peer around the centerpiece.

To raise the *kenzan,* use a small ash tray, a tea cup, a wooden block, a small cereal bowl, or whatever fits the bottom of the bowl. Does it show? Wrap it in waxed tissue paper or plastic wrap, or spray-paint it white.

Bulky materials are nice to use, but a nuisance. Driftwood, sea fans, sea shells, and plastic materials won't go easily into needlepoint holders.

Take a few minutes to wire two, possibly three, twigs securely on either side of the object. Allow the twigs to extend two or three inches below the lower edge of the driftwood or plastic object, and put the twigs into the needlepoint holder. They will stick.

Sometimes a ceramic container "sweats," which means the firing process was inadequate. That doesn't help the finish of the furniture. Spray-paint the bottom of the container with clear lacquer or heavy plastic spray, or brush a porcelain sealer on the back. One of the resin products would work also. See your hardware dealer.

If the problem vase is tall, remember it's not enough just to seal the bottom; the sides will need sealing too. A temporary solution is to coat the inside with melted paraffin. Be careful not to break the paraffin seal with sharp stems while arranging.

Even if a container is waterproof, rough ceramic edges should be covered to protect wooden table tops. Glue felt material to the bottom. Either cover the underside completely or cut several small, round felt circles to cushion the container.

5

Preservative Techniques

By following a few simple rules, money and time spent each month for fresh flowers can be reduced by one-third.

Where are you placing your fresh-flower arrangements? On the dining room table? Very good. But does your air-conditioning unit blow cold, drafty air across the flower blooms? Is your favorite arranging area the television or stereo equipment top? Waves of hot air come from them when they are functioning.

Both drafts and hot air dry out flowers. Leaves, stems, and petals lose the precious water that keeps them fresh looking. Add to the life span of your flowers and your own budget of time and money by avoiding these spots.

In addition to being careful where you place arrangements, you can prolong their beauty by conditioning. Proper conditioning is the real secret to long-lived flowers.

Conditioning

Conditioning is floral language for filling the cells of freshly cut flower stems with water. Soaking in water hardens them through a process known as osmosis.

To prepare material, use a wide-mouthed, shallow bowl, like a cereal bowl. Fill with water. Tamp the grouped stems of your flowers until all tips are even, and cut off an inch from all stems simultaneously, under water. Then, suspend the group in a half-gallon milk carton filled with cool water, adding a few ice cubes. Leave the blossom heads out of the water. Most flowers will become crisp and fresh in 30 minutes with this treatment, ready to arrange.

Fresh foliage should be conditioned also. Submerge leafy branches completely. For thin leaves, soak one to two hours; thick, leathery leaves, two to four hours. Since each plant is individual, test for crispness.

For plants that ooze a milky fluid when cut, immediately char the stem with a flame, candle or lighter, or plunge the stem ends into boiling water, wrapping the flower heads first in newspaper to protect them from the heat. Then plunge the stems rapidly into cold water following the heat treatment.

The quick, cold-water treatment is necessary because the heat of the flame or boiling water expands the cells; cold water shrinks the fibers. The result is that water is "pumped up" the stem, filling it with water, thus conditioning it. Time? Perhaps a few hours.

If possible always cut flower material early in the morning. At that hour there is still much water in the plant. As the day wears on the plant loses water and, therefore, needs longer conditioning.

After conditioning all materials, you are ready to make the arrangement. Fill a small bowl with water and keep it at your elbow. As you arrange, cut each stem again in water (fig. 20). Of course, your container should have water in it, so be careful of debris. It's difficult to fish out.

Commercial solutions are usually available at florists for keeping flowers fresh for longer periods of time. However, you can make your own preservative solution:

> 1 qt. of water
> $\frac{1}{4}$ tsp. Clorox
> $\frac{1}{4}$ tsp alum (potassium aluminum sulphate)
> $\frac{1}{16}$ tsp. ferric oxide (available at drug store)
> 2 tsp. sugar

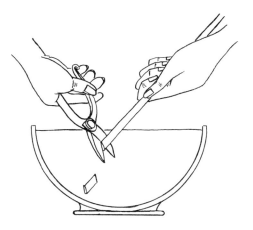

FIG. 20. Cutting a stem in water.

Use this solution in place of tap water in your container. After two or three days either change the water or add fresh tap water—from a height—to aerate.

If the tap water of your city is highly chlorinated, it may be wise to draw a bucketful and allow it to stand a few days to let some of the chemicals evaporate. Such a procedure brings tap water closer to rain water.

The following conditions carefully adhered to will give longer life to flower arrangements:

(1) Limit your flower material. Too many stems crowded into a vase inhibit water absorption.

(2) Remove as much excess foliage as feasible for artistic effect. Too many leaves cause excessive evaporation.

(3) Remove all leaves and twigs below the water line; they will rot and foul the water.

(4) Smog chokes greens as well as humans. Swish off oily dust in a sinkful of water to which you have added a few drops of mild soap. After swishing, refill the sink with cold, clean water. Swish again. Centerpiece materials must be carefully cleaned.

(5) Keep the level of water high in the container.

(6) A teaspoon of alum in the container water will keep leaves crisp.

(7) A charcoal briquet will keep water fresh. Use it in a tall, opaque vase.

(8) For a special effect in the evening, lightly spray the whole arrangement with cool water just before guests arrive. This gives a delightfully dewy effect. (Protect your table surface with towels.)

HINTS for FRESH FLOWERS

Some flowers need special care. Those used often in centerpieces are mentioned, alphabetically, with individual suggestions to keep them especially beautiful and long-lived.

ANTHURIUM: Sprinkle water on the flowers every day.

CARNATION: Rub dry boric acid into the cut stems.

CALADIUM LEAF: Rub salt into the cut end; give a brief immersion in tepid water. Score the stem with the scissors edge just as you would score a cucumber; then condition in cool water. Scoring helps the stem to absorb water.

CATTAIL: If you gather them fresh, putting them in water will allow them to continue growing. Depending on their stage of development, they may "explode" through their brown skins. To prevent this, dry them out of water for several days. Water-based hair spray may help to keep them from exploding if they are not too mature. Acrylic lacquer spray holds better, but lacquer may be detrimental to the cattail.

CAMELLIA: To prevent the flowers from falling, apply damp salt to the base of the stamen with a toothpick.

CHRYSANTHEMUM: Keep the leaves sprinkled with water.

DAHLIA: With your finger, rub equal parts of dry salt and alum on the cut end. These flowers will survive well out of water.

HYDRANGEA: Quick-dip the hydrangea in alcohol or salt.

POINSETTIA: Poinsettias are very difficult to keep from wilting as fresh, cut flowers. For those of you who grow them, try this method. Two or three weeks before Christmas strip all leaves from the branches you have chosen to arrange. Keep your choice to short lengths. The plant will heal all bleeding spots. Thus, when you cut the branch in three weeks there will be less shock to the bloom. Moisture will not leave so rapidly. Early in the morning of the day you wish to use them, cut the stems, char immediately with a flame, then plunge in cold water. Keep them in cold water for a few hours, then arrange in as deep a bowl as possible with lots of water.

ROSE: Dip stem ends in near-boiling water. Protect blooms. Condition in cool water up to the flower neck. Roses can be glycerinized; they will retain their freshness out of water at least two days.

SUNFLOWER: Dip the stems in vinegar for a few minutes.

TULIP: Dip the stem in a teaspoon of sugar immediately after cutting. When cutting flowers that wilt rapidly, carry with you a pail with a weak solution of sugar water. Sugar gives cut flowers quick energy.

Some flowers are impossible to hold past one day. In this category are day lilies, most hibiscus, and some spring flowers. Accept their limitations and use them accordingly.

EMERGENCY TIPS

DROOPY BLOSSOMS: Insert a toothpick gently into the center of the bloom, pushing through into the stem until the head is upright. The cause of drooping: improper conditioning.

DROOPY STEMS: Use a Kabob stick or a heavy wire inserted into the stem. If this fails, tuck the stem into a clear plastic straw.

FLOWERS OPENING TOO FAST: Choose one of three corrective measures:

(1) Wrap tissue paper around the heads while conditioning. Leave on until just before guests arrive.

(2) "Paint" inside of tulip petals, lotus, gladiolus, etc.

with slightly beaten egg white. Loop a twist of paper-covered wire around the head until dry. Remove wire; bloom will magically stay together.

(3) Tie a thread the same color as the flower around the head. Drawback: it is difficult to hide the line of the thread.

MESSY PLANTS: Examples: needles of the plumosa fern; autumn grasses; seedpods, such as milkweed pods. Use hair spray to hold needles and fly-away seeds on the branches and in the pods. Clear lacquer can be used with caution.

MUM PETALS FALLING? Drip a little cooling candle wax, temperature 110, on the back of the flower head. *Note:* When buying mums, tap the stem gently to check for falling petals which mark an old or diseased flower.

PREVENTIVE ACTION FOR FRESH BERRIES: Reference here is to berries on branches: bittersweet, huckleberries, pyracantha berries, etc. A water-based hair spray will keep berries from shrinking and wrinkling.

ROSE PROBLEMS: Revive by putting two inches of the stem in boiling water. Protect the blooms with paper. Leave them until the water is cool, then put back into the arrangement. Roses can also be preconditioned by immersing in cool water for 10 minutes—no longer. To keep roses at their prettiest stage, which is half-opened, insert a pin at the base of the petals to hold them fast.

ECONOMY TIP: Short-stemmed flowers are cheaper than long-stemmed ones. If the quality is equal, why pay for stems you throw away?

Weathering Wood

If driftwood, large or small, attracts you, would you like to know how to achieve that soft silvery-gray look that old weathered wood has gotten from lying on the beach?

Any wood can be weathered, even an attractive branch from the old fruit tree in the yard. Roots make attractive driftwood pieces too. Visit a site that is being cleared for

Plate 13
(p. 94) development; you may find several to choose from (plate 13).

If roots sound attractive to you, after a storm go out scavenging! Take with you a saw and a strong rope. Look for uprooted trees with many-branched root systems. Or look for blown-down tree limbs capable of being sculptured. There is no need to visit ocean or mountain. Don't haul any wood home unless it fulfills all your requirements.

If you go camping or on an outing, look for driftwood too. *Caution:* Be sure it is not rotten. Strike it sharply against a tree trunk to test. It isn't worth your time if it will disintegrate within a month or two.

Before weathering, clean the wood with a broom or brush if necessary. Trim off any excess twigs and saw off unwanted branches. Check to be sure there are no bugs inside eating away the heart of the wood. If there are, soak the wood in kerosene—outdoors, not indoors. Kerosene won't hurt your wood. After this treatment, start the weathering process.

Place the wood in the hot full sun for three to four weeks and soak it every day at least once with water. Use a hose. That's all.

Turn the wood every week so it will gray evenly. A garage roof is a good place for it to stay undisturbed by small children or inquisitive animals.

Warning: If you miss watering even once, the piece will take much longer to achieve the patina you want. And, of course, the sun must shine. Stay with it faithfully, you'll like the results.

Glycerine Technique

Glycerinized fall foliage is a wonderful nest egg to have. When treated with glycerine, fall foliage retains its beautiful coloring; it stays pliable and natural-looking and is usable at any moment.

Glycerine is a clear, viscose liquid available at drugstores in any amount desired. It can be bought in five-gallon tins, wholesale. If no wholesale outlet is available, wait for one-cent sales; you can get double amounts for that extra cent.

A commercial preservative can be bought, but making your own preserving solution is much cheaper and equally effective:

> one 4-oz. bottle glycerine
> 8-oz. boiling water
> Combine the two in a large empty jar.

Choose the piece of fall foliage you want while it's still on the tree, selecting one with some "character" to its shape. The best length may be about 3 feet, not too bushy.

Watch the tree closely in the fall. When the leaves are first beginning to turn, cut the branch. If you wait for full color, the leaves are too brittle. While processing in the liquid, the leaves will continue to deepen in color, then set for good.

For glycerinizing, follow the suggested method below with the above formula:

(1) Use only freshly cut materials, never any that have stood in water.
(2) Recut all the stems under water just before treatment.
(3) Place the stems immediately in the hot solution. Check to see that three to five inches of stem are submerged.
(4) Trim off any leaves under water.
(5) Allow the material to remain in the solution until you can see the shine of glycerine at the end of the leaves— maybe a week or two. Throw out the remaining solution.

Fall foliage is only one of many materials you can preserve. Experiment with your local foliage which may mature at different times of the year. For example, loquat glycerinizes to a beautiful deep chocolate brown in June in Hawaii. Other months, the same brown color is impossible to get. Loquat may be at the proper stage for glycerinizing in August or April in your home area. Always, for best results, pick materials just before the peak of their beauty. Experience will have to show you the moment.

The following materials have been glycerinized successfully:

aspidistra leaves	magnolia
beech	mahonia japonica
dollar eucalyptus	mountain ash
fatsia japonica	oak
holly	scotch broom (Genista)
hydrangea blooms	*ti* leaves
loquat	wild apple

A word of caution on the use of glycerine: Glycerine is sticky, so be careful with it. If too much is used in the formula, the treated material will "weep" drops of sticky ooze on the furniture during damp weather. It can easily be wiped up; it's just an avoidable nuisance.

To insure your investment of time and money in your glycerinized treasures, be sure to store them properly. They are invaluable for a last-minute crisis. To store after use, swish through a mild soap or detergent solution to remove dust. Not much soap is needed for dust. Shake material gently to remove excess water, tie the stems together with paper-covered wire, and hang them up to dry thoroughly.

When dry, cover lightly. Do not use an air-tight plastic bag because materials will mildew. The best way is to hang branches upside down from the ceiling of a storage closet. The next-best method is to use a proper-sized box. A florist shipping carton is good because it is heavy cardboard and is usually long and narrow. Some variety stores carry such boxes. Add charcoal briquets (five or six), moth balls, or mildewcide bags to absorb moisture and keep bugs at bay.

Other methods for preserving flower materials are:

(1) Oven-dried. Maintain the temperature of the oven at 200 degrees for several hours. Long, slow drying is good for fresh artichokes. Under treatment, they turn a very pretty beige color and keep indefinitely. Large branches obviously, are difficult to oven-dry. Experiment with grasses and seedpods.
(2) Electric iron. Press individual leaves. Put wax paper under and over each leaf before pressing. The only drawback is that the leaves often shatter easily.
(3) Silica gel, or similar borax and sand processes. This treatment is not recommended because you must handle the finished product so carefully. Flowers tend to disintegrate at a touch; the finished colors are quite pale.

Although you can acquire many lovely preserved materials through your own efforts, do take time to check preserved materials that are produced by commercial firms. They achieve colors in eucalyptus, for example, that are impossible for you to get. A wider selection of materials is available to them, also.

Japanese manufacturers process their materials in many ingenious ways. New methods mean money to them, and so they spend a lot of time experimenting. To locate commercial-type materials, try Ikebana catalogues or florist supply houses.

Plate 29
(p. 156) The dried, natural-colored edgeworthia in plate 29 on page 156 is one of the many commercial products produced for the Ikebana trade. Edgeworthia branches come in all colors and in several sizes. The average length is about 18 inches; some branches come as long as 4 feet. They have a resiliency that is used to hold the Triton shell in its upright position.

Some preserved commercial materials you may find interesting are:

bleached fern—all sizes, many varieties, in colors and
    natural beige
bleached fan palm—very beautiful, but expensive
bleached willow branches
bleached wistaria—all colors; many different shapes:
    curled, twisted, straight
bleached aspidistra leaves
bleached edgeworthia
dried grasses—check especially pampas grass
    lotus seedpods
bamboo splints—all colors, many different shapes of cir-
    cles, spirals, etc.

PART TWO
Containers and Equipment

6

Functions of a Container

Four Possibilities

If the container for your flower arrangement is merely an expedient to hold water, you do your home decor and your flower arrangement an injustice. If a container is worth having at all, it should contribute something of artistic value. Containers can function in four ways:

(1) as holders of water to keep flowers fresh
(2) as frames or backgrounds to set off arrangements
(3) as integral parts of arrangements
(4) as star features of arrangements

Using a container as a frame to set off an arrangement is the generally accepted function. Most flower containers on the market fit this category. As with a properly framed picture, a proper container is inconspicuous but effective. See *Plate 3* the arrangement of hanging bamboo on page 44 (plate 3).

A goal worth striving toward is to use a container and flower material as an integral whole. Artistically, there is complete compatibility; to a viewer, no other combination would seem quite as perfect. The Triton shell arrangement *Plate 29* on page 156 (plate 29) falls into this category. So does the *Plate 16* piece of driftwood with cattails on page 96 (plate 16).

Some of the ultramodern, free-form containers frequently act as star performers. The arrangement, of course, is built around the container, which often draws more comments than the arrangement itself.

If you own one of this type, keep the flower material simple in order to feature the container. One attraction per arrangement is enough. Simplicity doesn't mean just putting a flower in the vase; it must be the right flower arranged in the right way. Simplicity is true art where all but the essentials are pared away.

Simplicity doesn't mean blandness or innocuousness, either. The photograph showing the arrangement with the handmade pot from the clay of Jaipur, India, is an interesting example (plate 10). The container is a star-feature item. The arrangement gives the impression of a single unit, simplicity itself, with one giant allium and five safflowers, both fairly common materials. The unified impression is subtly different from what you would get using one material.

Plate 10
(p. 91)

Figure 21 shows the mechanics of anchoring the allium for this arrangement. It is not put in as a "head" for the vase, but is tilted almost at right angles to the mouth and held by a heavy iron skewer put through the stem. The stem is twisted and bent so as not to break in half.

A satisfying container always offers its owner inspiration. An example of such is the handsome, handmade wooden bowl; simplicity itself with no decoration but the woodgrain. Notice its use in two arrangements, one with the banana flower on page 43 (plate 2); the other with the kitchen scouring pad on page 50 (plate 9). Both are used in the second category, that of a frame for an arrangement. In the second picture, the bowl has been turned upside down to provide a base, a simple and imaginative use.

Plate 2
Plate 9

Through understanding the role of containers in arranging, you can help yourself to understand what you want from a container. You can evaluate prospective purchases or present possessions and choose discriminately rather than haphazardly.

Fig. 21. Allium stem and skewer counterbalancing a heavy head.

Discovering Containers

When it comes to choosing containers, you have four options:

(1) Make your own possessions do double duty.
(2) Improvise a container.
(3) Create your own.
(4) Buy one.

Selecting one of your possessions to double as a flower container makes good sense. It may be difficult to do, but give it a try. Remember, the first essential is something that will hold water or be able to take a water-holding unit.

One possibility is a large serving dish from your dinnerware set. How about some ordinary household item? Cigarette boxes with or without lids; bread trays or baskets of long, narrow, rectangular form have good shapes. There are cache pots with much charm, or jewelry boxes. How about ice buckets? Incense burners are marvelous units to work with.

Hobbies may give you ideas. Are you a rock hound? Glass slag holds a fascination for me; a chunk of crystal would be stimulating in a centerpiece arrangement. Would materials like quartz, marble, agate, malachite, or red granite inspire you?

Figures of animals have always been used for flower arranging. They should be fairly large: a ceramic cat, a large wooden duck, any of the fanciful wicker animals. To use, tuck flower materials into Oasis and hide the Oasis around the figure. (See Equipment, page 124.)

Plate 14
(p. 95)
The photograph (plate 14) shows a blue-enameled small candleholder designed to hold a large 3-inch beeswax candle. Check the arrangement carefully. It was photographed from an angle to feature the technique of holding a forked branch of the bittersweet through tension under the handle. Thus, no *kenzan* is necessary.

The arrangement can be made in a few minutes for a centerpiece. The airiness of the design and material makes it acceptable, even though the bittersweet curves higher than 18 inches. Since the bittersweet is long lasting, only flowers need to be changed for variety.

Coal was an unusual household item once used by a student of mine—not charcoal briquets, but actual shiny black coal. The student combined the coal with snow-white calla lilies, using no container. A cup pinholder hidden beneath the lumps of coal held water for the flowers.

Either in or out of a container, coal is an intriguing idea. By adding candles in holders, you might create quite an interesting, integrated table decor in black and white.

Out-of-the-ordinary possibilities are: a pencil holder from a desk set—waterproof it and add a small hook and use for a wall container; a straw hat (an interesting one from Thailand can be found in import stores); and sea shells, which you have probably already considered.

PLATE 10. Safflowers and allium in a Jaipur clay vase.

PLATE II. Maple leaves in a birch-bark container on a black lacquer base. The fallen leaf indicates late fall.

PLATE 12. Maple leaves and yellow freesia in a lacquered gourd, secured by a small kenzan and two sticks.

PLATE 13. Yellow dahlias, berries, and long narrow leaves arranged with driftwood and two orange pottery containers chosen for their texture.

PLATE 14. Chrysanthemums and bittersweet on a blue-enameled candleholder.

PLATE 15. Bunny tails and enkianthus in a Chinese brass iron.

PLATE 16. Two creamy roses with cattails and driftwood on black stones.

PLATE 17. Persimmons, a withered persimmon leaf, and small daisy chrysanthemums in a modern ceramic container from Japan.

PLATE 18. Red roses, pine, thin tapers, ilex serrata (a type of hollyberry) in a ceramic container.

Have you recently purchased some new terra cotta clay pots for planting a packet of seeds? Use them first as containers by temporarily waterproofing the holes in the bottom with paraffin. Three pots filled with flowers make a refreshing triple-grouping centerpiece.

A last household item could be mentioned. If you have a small oval wastepaper basket, recover it in brass or copper screening, thus completely changing its appearance. It might do as a wall hanging; use a plastic unit for water to keep weight at a minimum. Then, try only masses of greens for a nice effect with the shimmering holder.

Don't expect one household item, or any one unit for that matter, to do too many different jobs. If it does, the item becomes a gimmick, not an asset.

Finally, to reappraise your newly acquired household possessions, reassess each of them with three ideas in mind:

(1) as a possible container for flowers, already discussed
(2) as an accessory to a flower arrangement, hinted at in the hobby suggestions
(3) as a part of a possible mobile incorporating flowers, an idea that will be discussed later

Improvising Containers

If your possessions seem unlikely candidates for flower-arranging holders, maybe you can improvise. Surely someone gave you an oven-proof, clear-glass baking dish. Is it oval, perhaps 14 inches long? If the answer is yes, the dish is suitable for flower arranging. It also should be shallow, only about 2 or 3 inches deep. Such a glass dish was used one holiday season as a class arrangement. Here's what we did:

Spray the clear-glass dish (must be clear) with gold paint on the underside, not the top or inside. If you spray the glass on the underside, the paint shows through the high-gloss glass finish. This makes the dish look professionally gold-painted. Don't spray the sides with paint. That will show.

Let the paint dry thoroughly. Then spray the inside and sides with glue and sprinkle the wet glue with gold sparkles. Dry completely and, like magic, the baking dish becomes an attractive Christmas bowl! Add a needlepoint holder, sprayed gold. For flower material, use pine, red roses, perhaps red candles—a cheerful, inexpensive Christmas centerpiece.

Browse through the glass-dish section of the variety store. For a minimum outlay, you can have a large, unpatterned glass serving dish. Use it for serving, of course; but it can double for a flower container, either for floating arrangements (see water paintings), or for fruit and flowers. Also, it's a style compatible to the Peacock pattern (p. 140) if you solve the water-holding problem.

Very usable also are chip-dip trays and small glass ash trays. Purchase them in triplicate for a centerpiece, or buy enough for individual arrangements at each place.

Don't forget the plastics. Although they are a little more expensive, they are lightweight. A blue plastic plate would make a beautiful frame for flower arranging.

A stimulating field for exploration is the supermarket. Scan the grocery shelves carefully for intriguing shapes that hold food or cleansing agents. Apple-juice bottles, one of the many odd-shaped wine jugs, or saké stoneware are likely candidates. Can an empty cosmetic case you hate to throw away be refurbished for flowers?

Starting with a bottle or holder, change its appearance with a collage assembly in subdued colors; colored tissue papers or art paper are easy to work with. Spray the container with clear lacquer afterwards. Or wrap it with twine, colored cording, or raffia to conceal its origins. Try covering a jug with individual leaves from glycerinized fall foliage for an arrangement. None of the pasting, wrapping, or spraying is difficult or expensive; time-consuming, yes, but very rewarding in fun and sense of achievement.

Further suggestions for improvising containers are a little more elaborate. These items are slightly harder to find, but consequently more unusual and more challenging. An old iron lantern might fire your imagination. Depending on the style, use it either sitting on a table or for a hanging arrangement. Old Japanese roofing tiles have helped me in creating *morimono*. Are Spanish roofing tiles possible for you?

Hard to imagine, but found to be excellent through experience, are military shell canisters. They have a high burnished finish on them that is very attractive. Use a canister alone as a vase, or use it for holding water peeking through a 40-inch-tall wicker basket from Hong Kong. Wicker ware is inexpensive and fun. It takes spray paint so nicely.

Plate 15
(p. 95) As you are no doubt aware, household items can become antiques in the next generation. In plate 15, an antique Chinese iron made of a brass compound has been placed on a rosewood stand to give it elegance. Antique irons are collector's items for me. This small one, only 5 inches in diameter, has a particular charm with its bas relief decorations.

Creating Containers

Eventually, all flower-arranging enthusiasts create their own containers. To a beginner, it may sound complicated; actually, it is not. If you have tried any of the ideas so far, you have already created a container.

If we consider making a container from scratch, the most likely to suceed are driftwood containers. Fashioning a container from driftwood requires, besides the wood, only a wood chisel, polyethylene to waterproof the chiseled-out hole (preferably, you can line the hole with a waterproof resin product), a little patience, and a couple of hours.

The procedure is simple. Chisel out of the driftwood a hole large enough to accommodate a needlepoint holder; then waterproof the hole.

Plate 16
(p. 96) The container in plate 16 took 30 minutes to make. The driftwood was found as is, so no change was needed to make it balance. Only the hole had to be chiseled out; it's a small one for an inch-in-diameter needlepoint holder. The *kenzan* is clayed in permanently.

When you go driftwood hunting, to avoid disappointment in possibly a once-in-a-lifetime chance, be guided by a few simple suggestions.

(1) Choose chunky types of driftwood for containers, rather than the long stick shape. Chunk driftwood has larger areas from which to choose a spot for the hole.
(2) Be sure the wood is thick enough to chisel out. Examine it carefully.
(3) Be sure the wood is not rotten. This is very important.
(4) Be sure the driftwood "sits" firmly, no tilting. If not, you can make it stable by sawing off a portion. It must be stable. There is no point in dragging it home if it won't work.
(5) Clean the driftwood carefully before chiseling. Weather it if you wish.
(6) When chiseling out the hole, chisel small amounts of wood. Large pieces may split the wood. Slowly does it.
(7) If the driftwood won't make a table-style container, perhaps it will make a wall-hung style to use with dry flowers or glycerinized materials.

When waterproofing items for flower arranging, it seems elementary to point out that the waterproofing job should be done carefully and thoroughly so there are no leaks.

Many waterproofing materials are on the market; new ones arrive constantly. For driftwood, the fiber-glass equipment or resin products are good. Ask advice on the best article for the job. Everyone likes to give advice.

Although not strictly driftwood, old wood slabs can be formed into a container. Choose mulberry wood or any thin slabs of the distinctive, worm-eaten wood used for picture framing, keeping a rectangular shape in mind.

Good proportions for such a rectangular container are 16 inches long by 4 inches wide by 2 inches high. Waterproof by lining with a metal such as tin, or use resin again. Finish the wood by rubbing with linseed oil.

No one can ever have a duplicate driftwood or handmade wooden container. If you make one, it will be unique.

7

Buying a Container

Guidelines

Purchasing containers is a highly personal matter. Your choice should emphasize your special charm, and the container should function in harmony with all your home furnishings and accessories.

Traditionally, brides have wanted matched accessories, but today's bride mixes and matches with marvelous freedom of choice. Freedom of choice sounds easier, but actually it's more difficult. Getting accessories to match is simple; having accessories harmonize is much more challenging. Knowing what's available and the advantages and disadvantages of various types of containers may help to guide your choice.

The composition of containers is wide, using at least eight different types of materials. The largest assortment and the most varied according to shape, color, and size, is in ceramics. The most fabulous ceramics, star performer types, are created by artist-potters, but you can find many charming ceramic containers everywhere.

If you visit pottery factories, be sure to look at "seconds." Seconds are cheaper than first-line quality, and often the imperfections are minor. Thinking of minor imperfections reminds me of the typical Japanese philosophy on perfection.

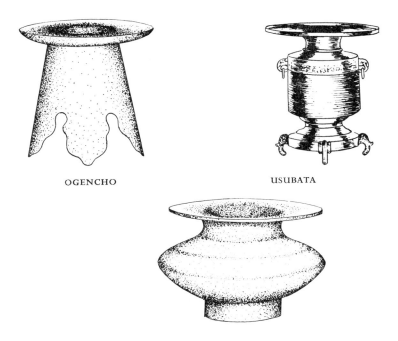

OGENCHO   USUBATA

FIG. 22. Classical bronze containers.

Ancient tea masters arranged the famous *chabana* to decorate the tea-ceremony room. Tea-ceremony flower arrangements are the highest form of pure Ikebana. Sometimes the tea masters purposely selected a vase with an imperfection to teach the students a special lesson in humility. Despite its flaw, the vase could still be useful in the world.

Metal containers are a second large category. All of these have high price tags, but there is no danger of breakage. Besides the familiar silver, brass, and copper, my favorites include the mellow pewterware and the beautiful bronze pieces. Many of the famous Japanese heirlooms, the *usubata,* are made of bronze (fig. 22).

The bronze classical *usubata* have two pieces, a platter-shaped top and an urn-shaped lower. Also two-pieced are *ogencho*, and there are other styles. Some are being reproduced today in iron. Iron is much cheaper but quite a bit heavier than bronze, and it also tends to rust. However, the rust is no problem; wipe over it with black shoe polish.

Glass is a popular category for containers. There is such a wealth of choices: new, antique, frosted, clear, patterned. Most countries have specialities in glass that make container shopping fun.

Clear glass has a technical problem for arrangers because all the stems show. You must arrange both above and below the water line. However, the self-patterned, abstract swirls of some glass products are strategically placed to make arranging easier. Shop carefully for glass.

Plastics have the same "see through" problem as glass, but they have an advantage in not breaking as easily. However, plastics do tend to show scratch marks so they need careful handling.

One of the most interesting categories is the basket-container. Its only drawback is not holding water, but that problem should be easy to solve. See Equipment, page 117.

Baskets are favorite containers for Ikebana, especially in the spring and fall. Baskets, just like bronzeware, become family heirlooms in Japan, and are handed down from generation to generation. The American Indian baskets may eventually come into this realm.

The wood category has already been discussed at some length. Commercial containers are made from driftwood, as you know. Commercial containers are also made of lacquer, which is balsa wood covered with lacquer coatings. The number of coatings determines the price of the article; the more coats, the more expensive.

Many beautiful wood containers, bamboo, cherrywood, rosewood, myrtlewood to mention a few, are on the market. Like baskets, they need some unit for holding water. Some Japanese wood containers are lined with galvanized tin. A simpler method, time-wise, is to use the modern resins if they will not ruin your article.

Briefly, the last category combines several exotic and rare materials from which containers are made: marble, soapstone, enamel, cloisonné. All are very interesting to use, but most are quite costly.

With this survey of the possible market, how do you go about choosing one basic container? A fundamental principle should be your guide—simplicity: of shape, decoration, finish or glaze, color.

We'll take a few minutes to check these four in detail. Simplicity of shape means no scallops, no flutings, no ruffles, no gold imitation around the edges or along the sides of the basic container. The vase should never look like imitation driftwood, imitation bamboo fencing, lotus flowers, tree trunks, or anything else but just what it is, a basic container for flowers.

Simplicity of decoration speaks for itself. Specific decoration can be a limiting factor. A vase with pine-cone motifs, for example, looks right with red berries and branches of pine; but summer flowers would seem inappropriate. Abstract decoration is preferable, but consider it carefully for its aptness with a wide variety of flower materials. It's more fun to have a wide choice. Highly decorated vases have a decided place in a collection, but hardly can be considered basic; perforce, they belong in the star-performer class.

High, bright glazes and finishes on containers are attention-getters. Shiny silver and bright brass are beautiful; know how you want to use them, otherwise these may be limiting factors for you. Pewter or bronze grow more mellow and beautiful with the years.

Special glazes on ceramics, lacquered baskets, or varnished woods all must be carefully considered for their possible use with assorted flower materials. Never lose sight of the general tenor of your other possessions; keep them all in artistic harmony.

Resolving the question of simplicity of color is perplexing. Just be reminded of the Ikebana way of choosing colors. To the information given you in the section on the artistic characteristics of materials (p. 40), I want to add one bit of know-how. The Japanese regard black highly for basic containers. If you have never tried to make an arrangement in a black container, you will be amazed how beautiful any flower material looks set off by the black color.

Likely spots to look for containers, other than pottery factories and shopping areas such as department stores, are antique shops, export–import stores, discount stores, and any convenient attic. Other areas to explore—the Salvation Army depots, interior-decorating shops, and thrift shops. Local bazaars, county fairs, and other such events you already know.

One Basic Container

The decision to choose just one container from the many on the market rests on the answer to this question. Would you prefer a star performer or a truly basic vase? It is a difficult choice. Base your decision on the type of home furnishings you own and your estimation of what you can live with for the longest time. Do not hurry yourself. Do not buy on impulse.

A basic container would be a container that could fulfill three of the four functions mentioned in the section on defining a container: it could hold water, act as a background, or be an integral part of the arrangement.

Specifications for one all-purpose container are eminently simple.

SHAPE: oval; length: 18 inches; width: 4 inches; height: 2 or 3 inches

DECORATION: none

FINISH: glazed, with a self-crackle pattern

COLOR: celadon, a subdued grayed or yellowish green of Chinese origin

COMPOSITION: ceramic, flat style, no legs, no foot, no high-pedestal stand

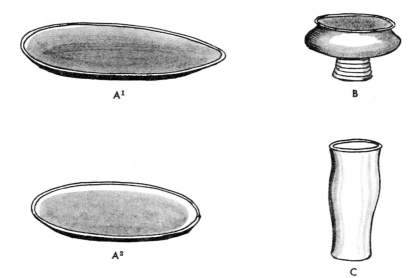

A¹

B

A²

C

Fig. 23. A set of three basic containers.

This would be a container beautiful to look at, easy to live with, versatile, challenging to the imagination, and aesthetically satisfying.

A Collection of Three

A frequently posed question is, "What would be a good basic collection of flower containers?" It's similar to being asked which handful of books would be the best to take to a desert island!

To be realistic for you on a limited budget, let's restrict the collection to three containers. Each of the three must be versatile alone and must also be capable of teaming together (fig. 23).

First container: either an egg-shaped dish of 16 inches in length, or a plate-shaped dish of 14 inches in diameter with flaring, not straight-up-and-down sides (A¹, A²)

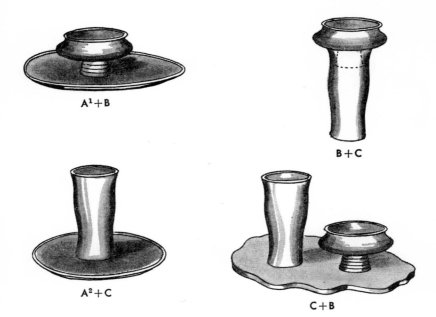

A^1+B

$B+C$

A^2+C

$C+B$

Fig. 24. Combining basic containers.

Second container: a compote style, simple in form, footed, approximately 6 inches in height, 5 inches in diameter (B)

Third container: a tall vase, approximately 14 inches high, with the opening of the mouth large enough to accommodate the footed base of the compote container (C)

If they are compatible containers (please note compatible, not identical) in proportion and color, then they might be combined in at least seven ways. In this circumstance, we would have the maximum usage of three containers (fig. 24). Compatible materials might be these combinations:

    (1) all ceramic
    (2) a combination of glass and ceramic
    (3) all wooden ware
    (4) all metals
    (5) all plastics or acrylics

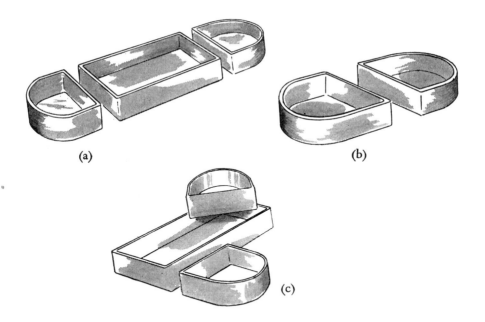

(a)

(b)

(c)

FIG. 25. (a) Basic containers; (b), (c) used in combination.

The Sogetsu school of Japan, for instance, offers a three-piece basic ceramic set, very usable for a beginner. This set is composed of one rectangular piece and two matching quarter-circle, arc-shaped containers, as sketched in figure 25(a). Each can be used alone or in combination (b) and (c). A similar pattern could be made in wood, if you like the design. Experiment.

To a basic grouping of three, you should very soon add an objet d'art, either personally designed or created, or bought for star-performer duty.

The last word on the subject of containers; take a friend, take your time, have fun shopping. When you find a container, enjoy its color, texture, shape, and feel. When arranging, show respect for it by leaving some areas exposed to view. If it's good enough to own, it's good enough to show.

8

Harmony of Flower and Container

At this point you should be aware of relating your flower material to the container. With identical ingredients, for instance, some cooks will make an excellent sauce, some an average one, others just a passably edible concoction.

What makes the difference? Proper handling and mixing. You learn through instruction or experience the deftness required for the first-class, smooth sauce.

For making beautiful flower arrangements, knowledge or experience is necessary. If your experience is meager, you need knowledge. Starting with the ingredients of material and container, two important concepts to keep in mind are harmony and contrast.

The chart on Relating Flower Material to Container has been carefully compiled (p. 198). It shows how these two important concepts are related in four categories to our ingredients. The four categories are shape, color, texture, and decoration.

Specific flower materials are suggested for a number of different, typical containers to help you to experiment on your own. The principles are so simple that they are easy to overlook in favor of something exotic; but they are the foundation of creative flower arranging.

Let's use an example and carry it through the four categories to show you how the principle works. Color determines choice for most beginning flower arrangers, so let's start with color.

For the container, we will choose the basic container suggested in the previous chapter, the gray-green celadon oval.

With this celadon container, choosing vivid deep orange gladioli for flowers, we would obviously have a contrast color situation. Check the color diagram.

If we chose to have greenish-white gladioli, they would identify perfectly with the celadon container; thus harmony, a monochromatic color combination. Easy. Now the next step.

If instead of gladioli, we choose to use a soft blue hydrangea for our flowers, we would have harmony with an analogous color scheme: grayed-green and grayed-blue. Grayed-green and grayed-blue occupy adjacent positions on the color diagram. If we chose deep blue liatris, we would have contrast with near opposite colors. The purple-blue of liatris is on the red side of primary blue. So much for color. The game has endless possibilities.

Blotting color from our minds, we turn to shape and texture. With the oval container in mind, spiky gladioli give us contrast; calla lilies, harmony. The calla blooms have a definite oval shape. The suggested basic container has a glazed finish; calla lilies are bisquelike in appearance. The shiny anthurium would be harmonious.

To set up a mythical situation and carry our example to an absurd conclusion, imagine our container having a bisque finish, oval shape, and greenish-white color. For decoration, a calla leaf is etched on the interior. Using calla lilies in an arrangement, we would have complete but not artistic harmony. No grace note here! Artistic harmony is a reasonable relationship.

Plate 17
(p. 97)
The arrangement in plate 17 is a study of harmony and contrast. Before you read the analysis, what relationships can you see? Check them against the chart, then read the following.

In the shape category, all is harmony. The shapes of flower materials are all round: persimmons are ball-shaped; mums are flat, but circular; the "ears" of the container are blunted flat circles. Note particularly, the two fruit among the flowers. They emphasize the rounded depth look of the massed flowers. The one fruit balanced on the branch is an exclamation point to "roundness."

The arrangement is deliberately shown in black and white to de-emphasize color. If you can imagine, though, the white mums are in sharp contrast to the brilliant orange fruit. Each mum has an orange-yellow center, and one fruit is near-ripe, with an orange-yellow tinge.

The heavy-looking container is grayish, like the bark of the persimmon branches, a small note of harmony. Most important, colorwise, are the flecks of ocean blue in the container. The brilliant flecks are the grace notes, the accent, of the arrangement. Reread the section on Ikebana color schemes.

In the category of textures, there is both harmony and contrast. Smooth, shiny fruit contrasts with rough pottery. The soft petals of the mums, neither shiny nor rough, bridge the gap between material and container. The withered leaf has the same highlights in texture as the container; the rough bark and rough surface of the container harmonize in texture as well as color.

On design, one small but important point: the line markings on the vase harmonize with the small parallel-line pattern of the double stems. Notice the two areas, one above the flowers, center left; the other above the hanging fruit, to the left.

The mathematical principle of proportion or scale can help you to blend your container and flowers successfully, The most difficult of all artistic relationships, proportion, can also be the most rewarding. Have you thought about proportioning flower material to a container? Or to itself? Or to your living room?

Mathematical measurements for the usual standard flower

arrangements are given in chapter 11. Even good rules, fortunately, do not stifle imagination. A concept of proportion contrary to traditional rules is used now in decorating. Called the "scale game," it may interest you, as it did me. Young designers have had much fun with it.

The "scale game" is the situation in which normally large things look small, and normally small things look large. A sample is the outsized figures from billboards used for decorating walls in homes. These pictures dwarf furniture, all ordinary household equipment, even the people living there. It's a temptation to try it with flower arranging.

For a party, you might try this scale-game arrangement. From a plant nursery, rent (if possible) four to six brand new, very, very large, clay flower pots. The number depends on the amount of floor space you'll need to cover. The tallest flower pot could be 18 to 24 inches. Get the tallest pots available, and set them carefully around the party-room area.

Fill the pots with several armloads of long, long field grasses, graduated in length. These should cost you nothing but a short trip to the nearest vacant lot. Obtain also, if possible, some colorful, long-stemmed field flowers to arrange with the grasses—cosmos have long stems. If you use fresh flowers, put a potato-chip can in your clay pots to hold water. Remember, clay pots have holes in the bottom.

Have someone hold the grasses and flowers in place while you carefully pile rocks and pebbles around to secure them. Use pretty rocks on top if you have them.

Dine sitting on the floor, and enjoy the Alice-in-Wonderland effect.

Most important, perhaps, in this matter of proportion is visual weight versus bulk weight for a flower arrangement. You are probably already aware of this concept.

Bulk weight is the actual amount of space taken up by a unit of flower arranging: for example, the size of a flower head, the length of the leaves, the container size, driftwood bulk, etc.

Visual weight is measured by how much attention the viewer gives a unit piece in the arrangement. The container might occupy the same amount of space as bulky driftwood but be less attention-getting. On the other hand, a flower may be a lot smaller than the container and yet be very obvious. Color plays a big part here.

Viewers will give a beautiful tropical flower such as the bird of paradise or the *musa rubra* (the gorgeous orange banana flower) immediate, strong attention. Not only color attracts the eye, but also unusual materials. Therefore, these flowers would seem to occupy more space than they actually do.

A burnt-orange, small container would appear to take up more area than the basic celadon oval container which is large but unobtrusive. A bright branch of fall foliage in the oval would carry much visual weight. The same branch in the burnt-orange container would have less visual weight.

Plate 17
(p. 97)
To test your "visual" sense, cover up the hanging fruit in plate 17, leaving the branch in space. Notice immediately how unbalanced the arrangement seems.

Now imagine the arrangement in color. What acts as a foil for the vivid color of the persimmon? The micalike blue flecks catching the light from the container are the balance element. Thus, you will understand why the fruit not only had to be there, but also had to be of that very eye-catching hue.

The combination of ripe persimmons and white chrysanthemums is traditional in Japan during the autumn season. The bright fruit hangs over the whitewashed walls of farm houses, with beautiful color effects. Fall Ikebana, quite naturally, include endless white mums and persimmons. Haiku poems feature this fall phenomenon, as do traditional scrolls and brush paintings.

9

Equipment

Only one set of "tools" is really important to flower arranging—the arranger's two hands. Sounds facetious. However, during years of watching Ikebana masters demonstrate their art, I have noticed this. Without exception, after preliminary cutting of the branches, each man used his fingers, never his scissors, to remove excess leaves or flowers. Asked why, the answer was always the same. "It looks as if the wind did it!" And it does.

Never mentioned by flower arrangers, but inherently understood, is the hard-to-explain rapport between the arranger and his flower material, accentuated especially by the sense of touch. The arranger has greater control over his flower material and greater rapport, through his fingers, than through a pair of scissors.

However, top-grade scissors *are* a must; they are basic equipment for major cutting jobs, for cutting stems cleanly.

Do not buy cheap scissors for flower arranging. Poor scissors mangle stems. They will not cut heavy branches. Their edges dull quickly. Poor steel will not take a honing job. Wait until you can afford a good pair of steel garden-shears. Buy those with smooth cutting edges. Good standard Ikebana equipment rarely goes on the bargain counter because it's always salable. If you see any at a reduced price, look it over carefully.

Use old sewing scissors, if you wish, to trim leaves evenly

or to cut out special sculpturing designs or damaged petals. Never use them to cut stems or branch material.

Holders for Shallow Containers

The other piece of basic equipment for flower arranging is the holder. Holders for shallow containers and for tall vases are quite different.

It's difficult to find a better holding unit for flat containers than the needlepoint holder, also called a pinholder or, as already noted, a *kenzan* in Japanese.

Advantages of the pinholders are many. They are easy to use. They allow for the precise placement and precise slanting of stems. They are widely available commercially in many variety, drug, or hardware stores. Needlepoint holders are reusable almost indefinitely. If the needles become bent under heavy branches, straighten them with a palette knife or a spatula. The best needlepoint holders are made of an alloy of lead. Those made of plastic are inexpensive but are a less worthwhile investment than the lead or copper types.

Other holding devices are chicken wire, metal cages, assorted plastic foams, and paraffin; also old newspapers, folded leaves, a type of clay. Nothing else has all the advantages of the needlepoint holder.

Needlepoint holders come in different shapes: circles, half-circles, narrow and wide rectangles, double and triple sets. Keep your container area in mind when selecting a needlepoint holder; buy the shape that fits best.

Needlepoint holders come in many sizes. The proper size for a flower arrangement depends on the amount of flower material you intend to put on it, not on whether it's big enough to hold the arrangement without tipping over. A large pinholder is difficult to hide with only a few flowers and a little foliage. The average size for an average arrangement could be about 3 inches in diameter.

A good *kenzan* to consider buying is the so-called sun-

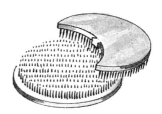

FIG. 26. Sun-moon kenzan.

moon Japanese style. It's a double holder which comes in sizes from 2 to 4 inches in diameter. Sun-moon *kenzan* give you two values: the sun to use normally as a holder; the half-moon for an extra holder in double-*kenzan* arrangements, or as a counter balance for a heavy arrangement. See figure 26.

For a beginner, claying in the *kenzan* is better than trying to counterbalance. With clayed-in *kenzan* there is no worry about breezes, curious animals, or inquisitive friends. The arrangement stays steady.

Clay-in is floral terminology for anchoring a needlepoint holder into a container with special clay. Floral clay is a product sold at florists' supply houses and sometimes at variety stores. Get the commercial sticky type, labeled Stickum or by other trade names, not the children's modeling clay.

Slapping a glob of clay on the bottom of a *kenzan* and hoping it will stay sometimes leads to disaster. There is a good method for claying in:

(1) All units must be completely dry: clay, hands, container, needlepoint holder.
(2) Roll or twist the clay into a long snake, a size smaller than your little finger.

(3) Coil it on the underside of the *kenzan* with a space in the center. The space acts as a vacuum to keep the needlepoint holder in place tightly. Exert enough force to anchor the needlepoint holder securely.

(4) To break the seal, pry it up with a spatula.

Melted paraffin can be substituted for clay. The drawback is the concealment problem. It's difficult to conceal an expanse of paraffin.

The *kenzan* is utilitarian, not an object of beauty. Although the Japanese feel it is unnecessary to hide fixtures, Western customs differ. Mechanics and fixtures should not show. Various ways for hiding the needlepoint holders are:

(1) Wrap the needlepoint holder in green or white waxed florist paper, not plain tissue. Tissue disintegrates.

(2) Wrap the *kenzan* in polyethylene or cellophane. A small sandwich bag is good. If you have difficulty in pushing the stems through the Pliofilm, use a pin or nail to puncture.

(3) Spray paint the *kenzan* the same color as the container.

(4) Use rocks, pebbles, stones, or sand. Use these items only when flower material and stones are found in the same general location in nature.

(5) Use marbles, marble chips, colored glass, etc. for special effects. Decorative arrangements have a different feel from nature arrangements, as suggested above.

Holders for Tall Vases

A narrow-necked tall container may not need any fixture, but most tall vases need something. Once you see the difference in the look of flower material resting against the side of a vase and the look of the same flower material using a fixture, you will always use a fixture. The holder makes flowers appear to spring from the center of the vase, fresh, growing, vital (fig. 27).

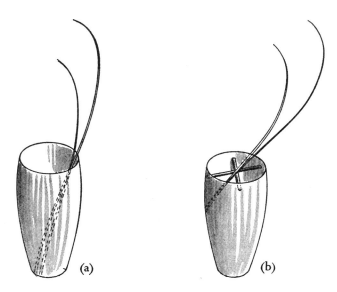

FIG. 27. Tall vases: (a) without fixture; (b) with fixture.

Holding units for tall vases where needlepoint holders cannot be used include chicken wire, forked sticks, special Japanese bamboo yokes, metal hooks, crushed newspaper, folded leaves, plastic foam, small, straight twigs, glass marbles, and many other contrived devices.

Adequate holders can be purchased to use in tall vases. Learning to make your own is simple and economical. Besides, it's always there when you need it. The easiest fixture to make, and the most effective to use, is two thin branches lashed to each other at their mid-points, called cross bars.

To make cross bars, you'll need your scissors and a branch about half the thickness of your small finger and the length of your arm. The extra length is for practice. Branches from hardwood or fruitwood trees are best because they will not split easily.

Judge how long to cut the twigs by measuring the container mouth. They must fit snugly and straight. No arching. If twigs are too small, they'll end up on the bottom of the container.

Cut the twig ends at a slant to fit against the sides of the vase smoothly. Place them one inch below the rim of your container mouth so they won't be visible (fig. 28). If the mouth of the container is very wide, try four bars instead of two, as in figure 29.

Caution: Twigs should be pliable, green—still living—and not too thick. Wet them carefully before putting them in the vase opening. Water makes wood swell. Your vase may suffer a chipped edge if the bars are inserted dry and water is poured into it.

For safe arranging, always fill the vase before you start. Water weights down the container so it won't tip easily—a good precaution. Water also helps preserve your flowers.

When arranging material, cut all the stems at a slant. Stem ends must rest against both the bars and the sides of the vase, not on the bottom, in order to achieve the graceful look of tall-vase beauty.

Balancing the flower material in the tall vase is the biggest headache. How do we do it? Mostly by testing. Slide the main branch stem up and down until you feel it balance. Or cut the branch shorter. Or recheck the hints on balancing heavy branches in the section on stabilizing techniques (p. 66).

For slanting or diagonal designs, keep the stems near the top of the container (fig. 31). This is also true for horizontal patterns. The higher the stem in the vase, the flatter it will be to the vase rim. The closer to the bottom, the more vertical the branch will stand.

Single-bar construction is useful for narrow openings and for lightweight materials. Lightweight materials could be spiraea, dendrobium orchid sprays, scotch broom, roses, many dry materials. Like the cross bars, the single bar makes flower material look vital.

To make the single bar, split the stem end of the flower material carefully (fig. 30). The slenderness makes cutting precarious. Insert a slender stick (the single bar) at right angles to the split stem. Lash together with wire. Measure,

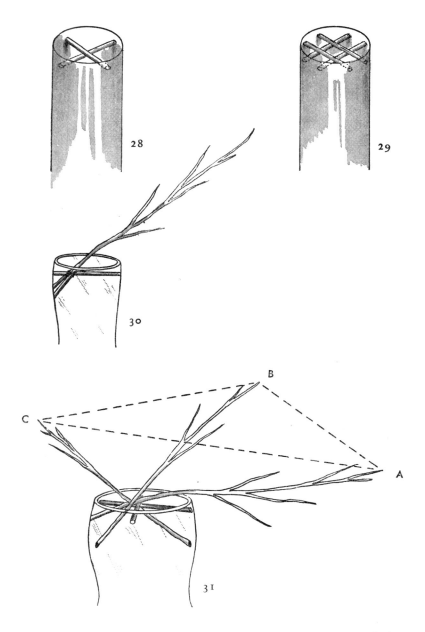

FIG. 28. Single cross bar.   FIG. 29. Double cross bar.   FIG. 30. Single bar.
FIG. 31. Three branches harmonizing in a Horizontal pattern. The branches are
wired to the cross bars, or to each other.

then cut the bar ends at a slant so that the bar fits tightly into the interior diameter of the container.

Instead of a slender stick, substitute no. 16 heavy wire. The wire does an excellent job of holding. Guard against scratching by slipping a thickness or two of paper between the wire ends and the vase.

General Equipment

Two products, both holding units, are good additions to your equipment. One is a marvelous, lightweight, water-holding foam compound with the trade name Oasis. Oasis is especially valuable for candelabra, wall sconces, mobiles, driftwood, flower sculptures, epergnes, or any spot where pinholders cannot be used.

Oasis comes in green rectangular blocks, which can be cut to any size or shape with a kitchen paring knife. Even soaked, Oasis crumbles easily, so carve it carefully. To insure more strength for heavy stems, wrap the Oasis in a piece of chicken wire before inserting the stems.

Soak the Oasis block in water for a few hours until it has absorbed all the water it can hold. Oasis floats when dry, so weight it down. When saturated, remove from the water and allow to finish dripping before cutting the shape. A thin plastic sheeting placed around the foam will prevent possible water-drip later.

With Oasis in place and its plastic wrap or wire carefully around it, you are ready to arrange. Don't put any branches in until you decide first where you want to place them. Then, cut and push the stem into the foam.

If you change your mind on flower positioning too often, you may have to use another block of foam. Stems leave unfillable holes; foam cannot be reused, a definite drawback. Foam is a little extravagant for one-time arranging unless, as pointed out above, it is the only solution for a holder.

Styrofoam and Oasis are not the same products. Styro-

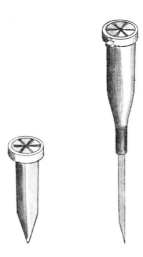

FIG. 32. Orchid tubes.

foam is a stiff plastic that doesn't hold water although its other properties are much like Oasis. Styrofoam is often used for dry flower arrangements in the same way that Oasis is used for fresh flowers—as a holding unit.

The other commercial product you should know about is the orchid tube, used extensively by florists to keep orchids fresh and securely anchored in corsages. These vials come in assorted lengths and sizes from 1 to 6 inches (fig. 32).

Orchid tubes are made of clear or green plastic. Each vial has a water-sealing rubber cap that permits stems to be inserted but no water to escape. Orchid tubes are perfect for single flowers with short stems high in an arrangement. They are easy to conceal and easy to refill with water; they are reusable indefinitely; they are inexpensive. The last plus factor is that concealment isn't too difficult.

The Japanese solution for a water-holding unit in baskets or lacquer or wooden ware is a small "cup" sliced from the giant bamboo. The cup measures about $3\frac{1}{2}$ inches across and is rather primitive but charming, and compatible in baskets. As you may know, the area between each node of bamboo is waterproof, providing there are no splits.

No effort is made to conceal these bamboo slices. They are put into baskets, a *kenzan* is added, the arrangement is made. Flower arrangers often devise their own holders for special problem areas. I have used water-filled, small balloons; small sandwich bags for liners; marbles; tin cans. Vegetables and fruits can be a temporary source of water, if necessary. Try grapes, apples, potatoes, oranges.

Perhaps for you a solution could be a small plastic container of some sort: an eraser box, a pretty ashtray—something that need not be concealed. Frequently, the solution to holding water for baskets and wickerware is a tin can sprayed to match, or sprayed black.

Other general equipment helpful for flower arrangers includes wire, cellophane tape, and floral tape.

Cellophane tape, you already know. Use it to keep a tip of a leaf in place, for one idea. Floral tape is a narrow, elasticized, papery sort of tape, adhering neatly to any dry surface. Obtain it where you get other floral supplies.

The tape comes in a myriad of colors. Florists use it to mask wire and floral "picks." Floral picks are small green sticks with attached thin wire used to strengthen flower stems. Use them as you would the sticks suggested in fixing techniques.

Wire ranks high on my equipment list for Ikebana. Wire is sold by weight, or thickness; the higher the number, the finer the wire. No. 30 is quite fine, a good weight for general flower use. Often you can substitute wire from vegetable packages or wire tucked into boxes of the clear plastic rolls. Use wire, for example, to mass flowers together; to attach wooden stick strengtheners to weak stems; to tape on the backs of leaves; to curve material; to insert into flower stems for added strength as well as curving purposes; to lash pieces of driftwood together.

Eventually, you may find a few additional tools are handy: a plastic-headed hammer, a small saw, nails, screws of assorted sizes, chisels, screwdrivers, pliers, a sharp knife, toothpicks, skewers, plastic straws, a small bottle of mineral oil for polishing leaves or pebbles. Many devotees of flower arranging resort to a tool kit for holding their assorted gear.

Not strictly equipment, but nice to have for several reasons, are flower-arranging bases and stands. They keep wood finishes free of damage from rough pottery edges. And, in addition to protecting furniture, bases have an artistic value. Often they give a tall vase the needed foundation for visual weight. Bases define the arrangement area and keep it isolated from a "busy" surrounding. Flower bases can also unify two or more containers, melding them into one decorative asset. Boards and bases come in a variety of shapes, sizes, colors, and materials. They are not difficult for a handyman to copy.

PART THREE
Patterns and Positioning

 10

Well-Known Patterns

To position "raw" flower material into a container, consider first the pattern you want to use, and the proportions of the material to container.

If you have not yet discovered the beauty and drama of two simple patterns, the Vertical and the Cascading, study figures 33, 34 (p. 132). Notice that just a few pieces of material arranged in either the upright or flowing style give a wonderful effect.

Beginners may need a little guidance in learning proportion. How do you take the measurement of a container? See figure 35 (p. 133). When proportioning flower material to a container, check the container "area," and follow these guidelines, below, for the longest (or highest) spot, A.

DOMINANT FACTOR IN ARRANGEMENT	SECONDARY FACTOR	PROPORTION TO CONTAINER
Flower material	small container	2–5 times
Flower material	large container	$\frac{2}{3}$–$2\frac{1}{2}$ times
Container (through color, shape, size, etc.)	any flower material	$\frac{2}{3}$–$2\frac{1}{2}$ times

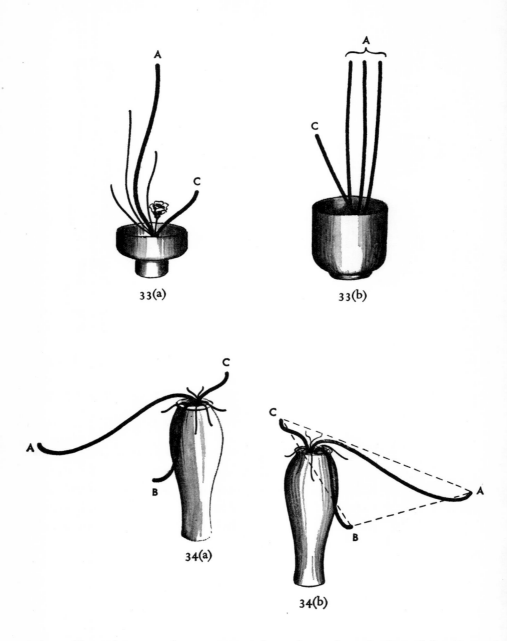

FIG. 33. Vertical pattern, front-viewing style, with visual weight (a) on left; (b) on right.

FIG. 34. Cascading pattern in a tall vase, front-viewing style, with visual weight (a) on left; (b) on right. Dotted lines indicate asymmetrical triangle points.

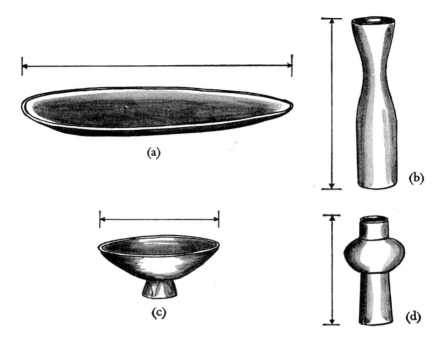

Fig. 35. The largest dimension of various containers: (a) length; (b) height; (c) diameter; (d) height.

In proportioning the other main points of an arrangement, use the Greek measurements of thirds. Cut the second main point $\frac{2}{3}$ and the third point $\frac{1}{3}$ of the tallest spot, A. These two subsequent points are designated as B and C in all sketches. Keep the helpers of all main points few in number and in artistic harmony.

Vertical Pattern

Applying these proportioning guidelines to the Vertical pattern in a one-view situation, use a small bowl to dramatize the feeling of height. With a small, low container of 5 inches in diameter, proportion the tallest flower four to five times the diameter. That's 20 or 25 inches in height. Try

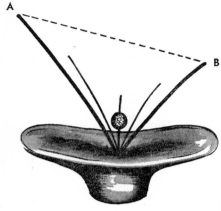

FIG. 36. V-shape pattern.

it before you dismiss the idea as impractical for you. If your low container is 12 inches in diameter and you plan a vertical design, measure the tallest material, point A, 2 or $2\frac{1}{2}$ times the diameter of the container; that is, 24 or 30 inches.

Plate 19 (p. 147) The photograph (plate 19) shows a vertical arrangement in a low container 7 inches in diameter. The tallest point of dry broom grass is 35 inches. The second main point, B, is 24 inches; C is 12 inches. In this particular arrangement, there are many broom helpers making the broom grass dominant; therefore, some of the bright blue larkspur flowers have been removed from the spikes. In your first attempts with vertical-style arranging, use helpers with discretion.

A useful variation of the vertical style is the V shape. The V-shape angle can be narrowed or widened at your pleasure. (See fig. 36.)

Plate 20 (p. 148) Harmonious blending of the V shape is evident in plate 20, with emphasis still on the vertical feel. The leaves of the cattails are clipped and arranged V fashion, lightly tied with wire to hold them in place. The daisies also form a V pattern, and the two small cattails in the bottom container give the final emphasis. The total produces a feeling of height. (Compare with plate 19.)

Cattails are easy to use for a first try. If possible, gather your own so that you can use the thin, attractive leaves; leaves are removed before florists receive them. Cattails grow profusely in swampy areas. Suggested substitutes for plate 19 are: pampas plumes for cattails and leaves; lavender or maroon mums or dry yarrow for daisies.

Plate 19
(p. 147)

FRESH FLOWERS FOR VERTICAL PATTERNS

agapanthus	delphinium
anthurium	Easter lily
bird of paradise	liatris
calla lily	narcissus
canna	stock
carnation	tritoma
clivia	tuberose
cosmos	tulip

FOLIAGE AND DRY MATERIALS
FOR VERTICAL PATTERNS

bamboo	ferns
birch logs	heather
broom	milkweed pods
bulrushes	nandina
nightblooming cereus	New Zealand flax
stems (cactus)	okra (seed capsules)
cycad fronds	pampas grass
dock	pandanus
dracena sanderiana	pussy willow
equisetum	umbrella grass

Cascading Pattern

Tall containers with cascading materials are not in general use by neophytes. However, to achieve the same effect, place your small bowl on a shelf above eye level, then use a cascading arrangement. Anchor the *kenzan* securely, please.

Plate 22
(p. 150)

The unusual latticed basket in plate 22 shows cascading material. A cross-bar fixture is used. Notice how drastically the normally profuse mock orange has been trimmed to show the beauty of the flowing line. Material is measured $\frac{2}{3}$ the height of the basket.

To analyze the proportions of this arrangement, recheck the guidelines. The basket is tall but it is lightweight in feeling, and so the flowing branches are dominant; the minimum measurement of $\frac{2}{3}$ the height of the basket is necessary.

With the same vase and different flower material, such as bittersweet, fern, or camellia branches, you may measure $2\frac{1}{2}$ times the height of the vase. The pattern could be horizontal, slanting, or upright. Allow a long bittersweet vine to partially encircle the tall vase for a Character arrangement in the flowing style.

If no tall vase is handy, substitute something. Camouflage a wine bottle with a collage or spray paint. Some bottles could be used "as is." Turn a tall wooden candlestick into a temporary container. Wire Oasis (wrapped in plastic) to its top; cascade flowers or vines. When you put material in the Cascading pattern it's easy to hide all the mechanics. Condition flowers carefully so they will stay nicely for as long as possible.

A list of common, easy-to-use flower materials that naturally grow in flowing lines has been compiled for quick reference.

MATERIALS FOR CASCADING PATTERN

bells of Ireland	honeysuckle vines
bittersweet	ivy
bougainvillea	leaves of the pampas plant
China root (smilax)	orchid sprays
fern family	spiraea
freesia	willow family
fuchsia	wistaria vine
hanging heliconia family	woodrose vine

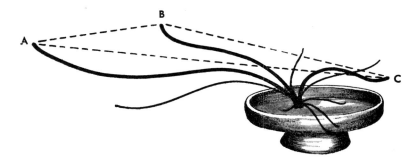

FIG. 37. Basic Horizontal pattern for table areas.

If the flower material you want to use doesn't ordinarily grow in a flowing line, use techniques to bend it. Remember that internal wiring can give you deep curves, if desired.

Horizontal Pattern

The Horizontal pattern also uses three main points. It adapts well to any container and to most settings, either On- or Off-table. When measuring, proportion the main stems to the container as mentioned in the guidelines for proportion, and see the Horizontal-pattern sketch, figure 37.

Take a little time to practice this pattern. It has two big virtues: first, it's less common than the vertical; second, it has great possibilities for centerpieces. (See centerpiece section for pattern variations, p. 176)

Plate 20
(p. 148) As you examine plate 20, think of your container rim as the horizon line. The visual point of interest will be just above the rim. Here is where you should put strong flowers to act as a balancing force to the long lines of the main points. "Strong" flowers mean those that are large in size, bright in color, exotic in species, different in shape, and so on.

The horizontal style looks well on any long piece of furniture. Set the container off-center sometimes. This style can look spectacular in a wall-hung container used for a buffet party.

Put your table against the wall. Hang a basket about two feet above the table. Use pink flowering cherry branches as main points, A, B, C. For the focal point, use one or two dark pink peonies, placed just above the rim of the basket and coming toward you. Lightly cover the lip of the container with lemon myrtle twigs for fragrance. Use shades of pink for table accessories. *Note:* If the weight of the branches tilts the container, put sand or pebbles in the bottom.

When a wall-hung container is used with the Horizontal or Cascading patterns as a centerpiece, always check to see that the focal point is at eye level for most guests as they approach the table to serve themselves. Such a centerpiece is not only different, but serves the practical purpose of keeping the buffet table uncrowded.

For a sit-down affair, do not use a wall-hung container in the same spot because the focal point would be too high. Lower the container approximately a foot and sit in a chair to check the viewing angle. Experiment for the best position for the container.

When using the horizontal design the first few times (with On-table arrangements) choose a footed compote like the one in the basic collection of three. The footed compote brings the horizon line away from the table surface and puts the focal-point area in good viewing position. A footed compote also gives you plenty of room to curve material without *Plate 23* striking the table top. (See plate 23.)

(p. 151)

If you are making a centerpiece rather than a three-view arrangement, the extra height of a "foot" helps to set the arrangement apart from serving dishes. By emphasizing rhythmic lines A, B, C and curving them below the rim of the container, sight lines of seated guests are blocked from the *kenzan*. In the photograph (p. 151) the compote holds a basic Horizontal pattern. Note that the flower ma-

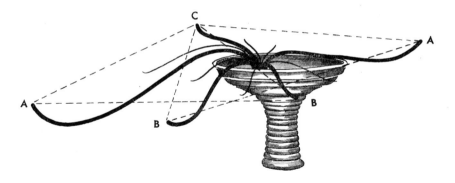

Fig. 38. Horizontal pattern in a tall compote for a centerpiece.

terial is not centered in the compote; it's positioned off center. An asymmetrical effect is aesthetically pleasing, a nice change from balanced compositions. Substitute roses, daisies, mums, or any garden flowers for the carnations. Grow your own hosta leaves. (See Plant Identification, p. 200.) For a large table, double the triangle (fig. 38).

To make the Horizontal pattern successfully, remember these three practical techniques for positioning. If positioning suggestions are followed carefully, more people will be able to enjoy fewer flowers—a desirable situation for the bride.

(1) Always place flowers and foliage with backs to the table top.
(2) Always set flowers low in the focal-point area.
(3) Set flowers with their faces looking up, not at diners or at the dining room walls. (Review the discussion of the "set" of a flower face, page 52.)

The Horizontal pattern is capable of infinite variations. It's one of the best patterns to use for Character arrangements because it accommodates personalized touches.

Peacock Pattern

The Peacock pattern, as you can readily see in figure 39, is established on the familiar radiating lines. The idea sprang from a trip to India where I saw wild peacocks along the roadside spreading their tails in breathtaking beauty.

With various materials and containers, this design is capable of many different moods. The container sketched in the illustration of the pattern is a platter type. However, any plate will suffice as long as it can hold two inches of water and is free from distracting decoration. Notice how easy the pattern is to make.

STEP ONE: Use only five leaves for the fan. Choose them unblemished. Place precisely. Cut the middle leaf about 18 inches high; the two flanking leaves 16 inches; the remaining two 15 inches.

STEP TWO: Place two additional leaves for "tail" feathers at right angles to the fan. This simple step gives your arrangement instant perspective.

Caution: Always cut the two tail pieces approximately $\frac{2}{3}$ the length of the tallest fan piece. The fan and tail pieces should be of identical materials.

STEP THREE: For "head" view, choose short materials. Suggestions:

(1) piled up rocks, pebbles, sea shells

(2) short greens; ferns, asparagus, etc; wire into small groupings

(3) short flowers; wire into small groupings

(4) blooms; if you plan to use stems of flower materials for the Peacock radiating lines, use the blooms for the "tall" area. Attractive stems are calla lilies, agapanthus, allium, umbrella grass

STEP FOUR: To complete the arrangement, fill empty sections with five to seven flowers having abundant leaves: roses, marigolds, zinnias, marguerites. Cut them varying short heights to keep the emphasis on the peacock design.

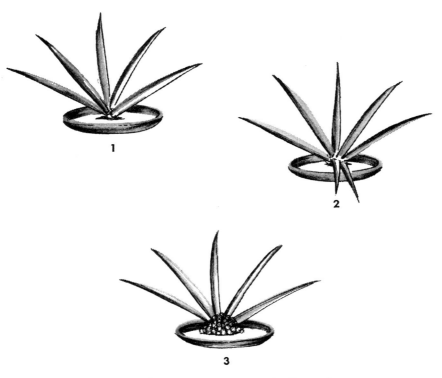

FIG. 39. Three steps in creating the Peacock pattern.

The temptation with the Peacock pattern is to use too many flowers as fillers for "empty" spots. Keep open space in the arrangement to point up the flowers you do use. Fewer flowers are better artistically.

Recheck the photograph on page 45. Note how the narcissus flowers are "looking through" the leaves for a three-dimensional effect. They are used in this fashion so that the arrangement will not have a segmented look. Flower materials should meld.

Flower materials for the Peacock pattern need one characteristic, beauty from the tip to the base of each stem. Beauty can include smoothness, roughness, knobbiness, attractive color, ribbed qualities, or whatever other engaging feature you like. Some materials have "interest" clustered at the top, such as bunny tails; others have interest all the way down the stem like the pussy-willow wands.

The commonplace materials suggested below are suitable for the radiating-line Peacock pattern. They are long lasting, in some cases even permanent, so only flowers need be changed. And they are easy to use, too.

MATERIALS FOR PEACOCK PATTERN:
RADIATING LINE

blackberry-lily leaves	gladiolus leaves
broom grass	iris leaves
bulrushes	moth mullein (dry stalks)
bunny tails or fox tails	narcissus leaves
calla lily stems	pussy-willow wands
equisetum	wheat heads (fresh or dry)

The Peacock pattern can be made with a solid-appearing material for the "fan," which is a simple style to arrange. Cut the leaf stem very short and anchor it in the *kenzan*. Add flowers and pebbles.

Large, pretty leaves are perfect for two-view positioning, so look for material that is attractive both front and back. If you don't like the "back" look, modernize. Spray paint it with color.

MATERIALS FOR PEACOCK PATTERN: FAN SHAPE

fatsia japonica leaf
monstera leaf
philodendron family of leaves
palmetto leaf
lady palm leaf
sea fan
some manufactured or treated materials

Several of the following materials originate in tropical or

Asian regions. If you can't find them locally, look for them when you travel. Shopping for indigenous materials in a foreign country is much fun.

FOLIAGE AND GRASSES

allium stems (straight)
bamboo roots (straight, and very clean; Japan)
fan-palm leaves (tropics)
papyrus stems (giant or miniature)
sugar-cane stalks (thin, new, red color; Hawaii)
swamp grass (glycerinized: curly or straight; east coast, U.S.)
tambo-broom grass (Philippines)
teasels
volcano grass (Hawaii)

FRESH FLOWERS

delphinium	snapdragon
larkspur	tritoma (straight stems)
liatris	tuberose

MISCELLANEOUS

coffeeberry sprays (rainbow colors of orange-red; perishable, but will dry in time)
dry palm clusters (cut apart; use singly)
pyracantha berries (U.S.)
sea-coral fingers (Philippines)

11

Ikebana Inspirations

Two ineffable charms set apart an Ikebana from a general flower arrangement. One charm is the achievement of a three-dimensional look; the other charm is the manner in which water is used.

Three-Dimensional Quality

A flower composition without a three-dimensional effect is plain and ordinary, with little grace or elegance. The three-dimensional look is hard to recognize in a two-dimensional picture, but let me point out ways to "read" a picture in order to appreciate three-dimensional qualities.

Ikebana have height, width, and depth. The use of thickness is different from that in ordinary flower arrangements. The Japanese word for thickness is *atsumi*. An Ikebana must have bulk (thickness) with a "see-through" quality.

Recall flower arrangements you have seen that have similar qualities of height, width, and depth. Depth is achieved often through mass. Flowers are very thick; in fact, they are so thick that they are impenetrable to the eye. The visual effect is really that of a plane surface, or two dimensions, height and width. Depth is lost in mass.

Plate 28
(p. 155)
In plate 28 the 3-D technique can be seen even though three large sunflowers are massed in a narrow-necked container. Notice that each sunflower angles in a differ-

ent direction. The expedient of gently curving the high cattail leaf over the flowers shows depth immediately, even in a picture. You can have 3-D in your arrangements too. The following paragraphs analyze it specifically, showing you how to lift flower material into space, both at the rear (depth) and at the front (perspective).

Attain depth by cutting flower material short at the back of your arrangement; the back is the point in space farthest away from the viewer. Things at a distance look small.

Frequently, Western flower arrangements place flower material tall at the back, which is a beautiful way to arrange. For variety, try the Ikebana depth principle. It can be used with any of the patterns discussed in the book.

The most fascinating application of the depth principle could be to the centerpiece. Place flowers, cut short, in the center of the arrangement (focal area), since logically the center is the farthest point from all viewing sites. This idea is contrary to all generally accepted methods of centerpiece arranging. Flowers are usually placed tall in the center, tapering off to low points on either side.

Perspective is the twin 3-D factor to depth. Perspective is the line along which the eye travels in space from a point in front of an Ikebana. Its use is effective in good Ikebana, although critics sometimes comment that materials in tall-vase arrangements seem to be "falling out" of the container.

Proper use of perspective branches, with enough visual weight in the body of the arrangement, will obviate this feeling. Like depth, perspective can be used in a center-piece. Where? In the small areas where stems come over the rim of the container. Place them carefully. Don't allow branches to hang over, or lean on, the edge of the container.

Three-D can be applied to even one piece of flower material. Here's economy again. If you want to use just one pussy willow or one piece of scotch broom, plus a flower, bend the foliage as outlined below. The following method cuts space two ways and avoids the flat look that many curved branches have.

STEP ONE: Bend lower $\frac{1}{3}$ of the branch down in a gentle curve.

STEP TWO: Bend upper $\frac{2}{3}$ of the branch up in a gentle curve. (These two steps have already been outlined in chapter 4, p. 58.)

STEP THREE: Bend mid-branch toward the chest to a desired gentle curve. This is the 3-D bend. Apply prudence. Bend different areas of the branch for the back-front rhythm. Be sure that opposing curves blend into one another. Make no abrupt directional shifts.

Try curving spiraea in 3-D fashion. Any fresh or dried vine is good.

Another way to achieve a 3-D look is the *fukami* technique. *Fukami* translates as "seeing something through a mist or veil." Psychologists comment that something seen through a veil or mist seems to hold much more fascination than a completely exposed object. Japanese Ikebana have this air of allure, the "peeking through" charm.

Plate 27 (p. 154) The veiling technique is illustrated in plate 27. The glimpse of red dahlias and five green equisetum through snowy gypsophila is quite intriguing.

Flowers can be "veiled" with many materials. Lacy fern, palms, any pierced material—all are good. If you can't find *Plate 3 (p. 44)* veiling material, cut one out. See plate 3.

Stylize material by removing some of the leaves, by cutting fronds short, by removing some of the internal flowerettes of a clustered group, or by cutting holes to make graceful air spaces. Experiment with baby's breath, tumbleweed, filmy statice, patrinias, palm, thinned-out pine needles, and bare branches.

Water Charm

The importance of water and water surface in flower arranging is underestimated by most Western arrangers who use water mainly to keep flowers fresh. Arrangers of

PLATE 19. Variegated broom grass and larkspur in a copper iron.

PLATE 20. Daisies and cattails in two of the triple basic containers.

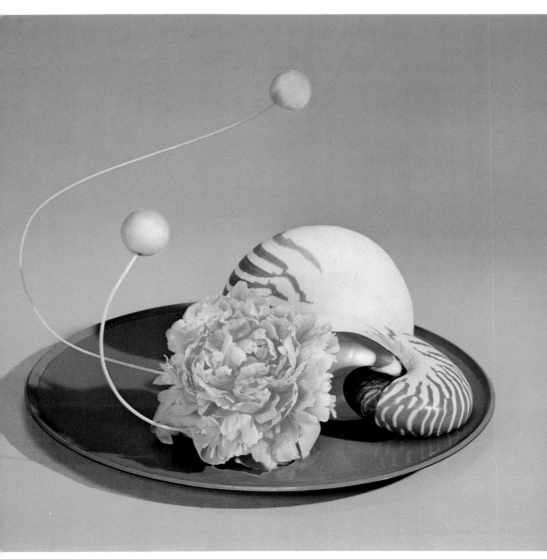

PLATE 21. A peony, two nautilus shells, and two balls on a lacquer platter.

PLATE 22. Pine branches and white mock-orange in basket.

PLATE 23. Carnations and hosta leaves in a footed compote.

PLATE 24. Three cosmos in a glass dish.

PLATE 25. Six bleached fern leaves with short branches of Philippine woodroses, three white mums, and seven palm fruits.

PLATE 26. The preceding arrangement (Plate 25) viewed from the upper-left corner to emphasize depth.

PLATE 27. Red dahlias and green equisetum with gypsophila in a blue glass container that highlights the materials through its contrasting bulk and color.

PLATE 28. Sunflowers and cattail leaves in a red-orange narrow-necked container.

PLATE 29. Starlilies, sunflowers, common aralia leaf, and bleached edgeworthia in a ceramic vase, with a 14-inch Triton shell.

PLATE 30. Persimmons, mums, and a moss-covered branch in a ceramic dish—a small island at a river bend in early October.

PLATE 31. Driftwood, copper mesh, cymbidium-orchid spray, and azalea greens make a perfect two-view arrangement for an entry-way to a home.

PLATE 32. Camellia and pine arranged in a hollowed-out, lacquered gourd. The black interior sets off the flower material.

PLATE 33. Pine, mums, and a candle in a bright golden glass boat—a Christmas arrangement.

PLATE 34. Easter lilies, pine, and wicker strips in a flower sculpture.

classical Ikebana have always considered water an integral part of a flower arrangement, and they show it off equally with flower material. Water is a beauty element. Have you tried accenting the water surface with flower materials?

Plate 24
(p. 152) In plate 24, three blossoms of the common cosmos are floated on clear water to emphasize the water surface and to give a cool feeling. In addition, the water sets off the beauty of the petal formation, a rarely considered aspect of the cosmos.

Wouldn't it be effective as a centerpiece on a dessert bridge table for four? The container is only eight inches square. Use glass plates for serving the dessert and coordinate your colors.

WATER PAINTING

Ukibana, the water-painting arrangements of Japan, offer intriguing ideas to feature water. The word literally means floating flower.

Ukibana started centuries ago, so the story goes, when a famous general handed a flower master's daughter a branch of peach blossoms and asked her to arrange them. Having no holder, she plucked off the blooms and floated them on the surface of a water-filled container. With her ingenuity, floating flowers were born in Japan.

The paramount feature of water-painting style is the beauty of water; its sparkle, its movement, its cleanness, its coolness, and, lastly and subtly, man's need for it.

To arrange a basic *ukibana,* imagine the water surface as the canvas. As an artist uses paints, use flower material to make a design in the container. With water featured, not much material is needed, but what is used must be carefully chosen.

Study the cosmos arrangement again. Notice that each cosmos has an individual characteristic. These particular ones were chosen from a mass of blooms.

The most striking and appropriate material for *ukibana* would be material from a water-growing plant. Water lilies rest on the water surface in their natural habitat. Lotus also grows in water; hydrangea's name is derived from the Greek term meaning water.

Otherwise, choose flowers and leaves for exceptionally beautiful color or for unusual formations. Land flowers that look well against water are cosmos, dahlias, daisies, and calendulas. Think, too, about filmy ferns or asparagus tendrils as "veiling" materials to enhance water.

If you cannot find something unusual in flower material, use a pretty bloom and add a Character element. Character elements compatible with water are: Petosky stones, moss agates, a small figure like the little, unobtrusive green jade turtle in the photograph. Did you discover him before? An unobtrusive element discovered by a viewer always gives added delight.

Still at a loss for material? Take a trip to a botanical garden. Note what flowers and plants grow at poolside areas; these will tell you what grows in your area.

Don't be restricted to one or two flower blooms. Try massing delicate blooms together. Gather many sweet peas or violets. Using a short section of a pencil as a center post, wire stems around the stub. If you take some care, the unit will stand alone; if not, use a pinholder. Then lay a necklace of coral beads gracefully through the water. Coral beads are an abstract Character element but, again, a material whose origin was water.

In a true *ukibana*, air currents move the floating flowers around in a natural fashion; the design constantly changes. This may or may not be to your liking. Sometimes my preference is to keep a prearranged design stationary—a water painting, rather than an *ukibana*.

Plate 21
(p. 149)
The water painting in plate 21 has a feeling of water currents and the sea generated through the rhythmic curves of the stems of the green balls.

Mechanics for water paintings require only anchoring the pinholder with clay and cutting the stems of flowers straight across, short enough so they will balance well.

Low, shallow containers show off water to the best advantage. The pale green celadon container would do well for water paintings, as would the plate or egg-shaped container. Containers of clear glass or plastic are especially effective since they make water appear infinite.

On the other hand, containers of stone, marble, cork, lacquer, or pewter give a contrasting weightiness to the fluidity of water. You can appreciate the fact that the look and feel of a container add immeasurably to the beauty of a water painting.

For you, the bride, these arrangements have special values. Few materials are used. The arrangement can be created in your mind as you home come from work. It can then be executed quickly.

Candles always add magic to water; candlelight and water are surefire beauty. When using candles, try to incorporate them into the painting area with tiny individual holders, or carefully place them on a *kenzan* rather than standing them outside the arrangement.

Note: To fasten candles on the points of a *kenzan* without splitting the wax at the base, take a lighted match and warm the candle bottom. Then quickly push it onto the needles and hold until the candle wax is firm again. The candle will stay put.

Ukibana should be used in small spaces where people can see them close-up—another plus value for newlyweds. *Ukibana* also will never obstruct cross-table conversation. In fact, *ukibana* might become a conversation piece. For a fun party, buy two small, orange-colored, live goldfish at your local dimestore. Add to your water painting.

WATER-VIEWING

Water is also a paramount feature of a second Ikebana style, the water-viewing arrangement. In a water-viewing style at least half the water area in the container is exposed. What's the difference between *ukibana* and water-viewing?

Water-viewings aren't made flat to the water surface as

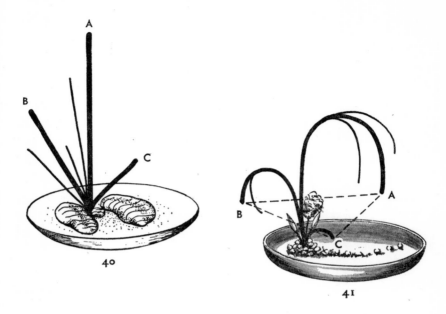

FIG. 40. Vertical pattern with water emphasis using flat stones.
FIG. 41. Cascading scenic arrangement.

are *ukibana*. Unlike those in an *ukibana*, materials generally go outside the confines of the container.

Water-viewing styles give the viewer the feeling that he is actually standing at the edge of a riverbank or a woodland pool, or by a lake or a garden fountain. Scenics always resemble a place you remember or a place you'd like to be. Viewers identify. The best patterns are vertical and diagonal. Japanese arrange these "scenics" as front-viewing styles. However, when all-flowers are used with the split *kenzan,* a nice centerpiece results.

Use water-connected materials: iris and iris leaves; narcissus and narcissus leaves; lotus and leaves; agapanthus; bulrushes; clipped umbrella grass; star of Bethlehem; any of the many varieties of lilies. Follow either of the two patterns sketched in figures 40 and 41.

Patterns and Positioning 164

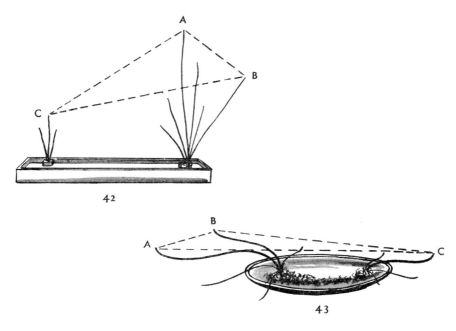

FIG. 42, 43. Double kenzan arrangements: vertical and horizontal.

Since Ikebana scenics are conceived as natural settings (lakes, ponds, rivers, etc.), there are "islands of vegetation." Hence, you need additional *kenzan*. Two islands mean two areas separated by water. Figures 42 and 43 show patterns using two needlepoint holders.

Multiple *kenzan* can be used to give the effect of a bend in a stream, such as is evident in the photograph of persimmons and daisylike mums (plate 30). Five needlepoint holders anchor the material.

Plate 30 (p. 157)

When using two *kenzan*, separate them as widely as possible in the container. There are several subtle techniques to give the illusion of one island being at a distance, thus providing a three-dimensional quality to the water-viewing style.

(1) Use a large group of flowers on the "near" island.
(2) Use sparse material on the "far" island.
(3) Cut sparse material very short to give a distance look.
(4) Use different foliage on the "far" island.
(5) Cut materials for both islands short on the center-of-container side of the *kenzan;* cut long over the edge of the container. The technique will make the water area between the two needlepoint holders seem to be in a hollow between two stream banks.
(6) Use techniques for all patterns: vertical, horizontal, or diagonal.

Water-viewing arrangements lend themselves to driftwood and to old, heavy, mossy branches. Remember, to a Japanese a gnarled branch gives strength, age, and dignity to arrangements. When you understand this philosophy, using "dead" branches becomes meaningful.

One typical Japanese arrangement, created each season just as we put up the Christmas tree, is the "water-diving plum." The main material is always an old, flowering, mossy plum branch. A slender off-shoot dives into the water of the container; its tip, in bloom, rises gracefully from the water several inches from the point of entry. No flowers are ever left on the underwater part.

Would you like to create an effect of walking down a garden path? An all-flower arrangement? Use the Vertical pattern, figure 40. To keep natural harmony, use not more than three different types of flowers and only those that normally grow in the same habitat. Use stones or pebbles to heighten the impression, placing them in as natural a way as possible; don't just dump them into the bowl.

How can you think up a water-viewing arrangement? Recall any scenery that you enjoyed in the past; pine branches against the mountains, or tall tree trunks in a forest area where you felt pleasantly dwarfed, or a rocky hollow with moss and a swimming area; or just a walk in a beautiful arboretum.

The next time you go on a picnic bring home a small rock, an interesting branch or root (from a storm-uprooted tree!) to be your inspiration. Paintings, photographs, and calendars—as well as memories—help.

When creating water-viewing or water paintings, be sure no debris such as leaves, bits of branches, twigs, flower petals, or bugs clutter the water surface. Tepid, stagnant-looking water has an adverse effect on anyone viewing such a scenic composition.

Nature's Seasonals

Holidays are times of the year when flower arrangements are particularly important. All of us associate certain flowers with certain holidays: pine for Christmas, roses for Valentine's Day, and so on.

Classical Ikebana designs include prescribed ways to arrange flowers, foliage, and fruit that show the growth progression of a plant. Spring is the favorite season of the year. Man's joy at seeing new growth, beautiful flowers, and the wealth of flowering branches inspires some unique Ikebana.

One of the most famous series is that using the Japanese iris and its leaves. Cultivated extensively, iris grow over much of the year in Japan. During the best showing season, June, the Emperor goes to Meiji Park in Tokyo to view the famous river of iris.

Established ways of arranging iris leaves and flowers are highlighted in the following paragraphs.

EARLY SPRING: The major feature of the iris plant in early spring is its leaves. Therefore, early spring arrangements feature leaves, no flowers. One or two buds are included as a promise of the coming beauty. Leaves are placed very tall, very precisely.

MIDDLE SPRING: Buds are tall; two may be in half bloom. Each piece of material, again, is carefully placed. Green leaves are abundant, clean, and sparkling from spring rain.

LATE SPRING: Flowers are tall and in bloom. Only a few buds are coming up through the leaves. Leaves are shorter, less in evidence, but still green and fresh. All materials are carefully placed. Lots of water is showing, and pebbles are used.

EARLY SUMMER: Many fully opened iris are now available with no buds showing. Leaves are curling, fading. This curling is shown by the arranger, who curls the leaf tip around his finger.

LATE SUMMER: Iris seedpods are used high in the arrangement. This is a different arrangement of iris from spring, with few leaves, fewer flowers.

Using flower materials to represent nature's timing could add another facet for your imagination to explore. The style would need some knowledge of plant life, but it's fun learning. Watch a favorite plant through a growing season.

An interesting plant cycle to observe is the artichoke's. Leaves, buds, flowers, seedpods, and fruit all have appeal. All parts are usable in flower arranging. Try growing this vegetable and see.

When arranging, use the flowers and leaves from your own plant. Purchase the fresh fruit because it's a little hard to develop. Also, purchase the dried seedpods, called cardone puffs; they keep indefinitely. Don't forget you can preserve fresh artichokes for later use by the oven-dried method.

Below are suggested seasonal groupings. Some are unusual combinations chosen from Japanese traditional arrangements; some have similar growing habitats or similar blooming times. Other groupings are chosen for color, some for shock appeal. Whatever change you make in the original combination, consider it a creative effort. (Places listed indicate growing areas in the world.)

SPRING:

(1) Acacia and daffodils (temperate zone). Use in a yellow

container. Find one astringent note for a Character element to offset the yellow colors. Something in lime?

(2) Pussy willow and hydrangeas in a water-viewing, multiple-*kenzan* pattern. Model after plate 30. Grow your own hydrangeas, then glycerinize.

(3) Tulips and flat, black, beautiful stones. No container. Hide the *kenzan* under the stones (shock appeal).

EARLY SUMMER:

(1) Liatris in the Peacock pattern. Mass pale lavender, small mums. What color container?

(2) Three birds of paradise and five leaves. Put into vertical style with birds tall. Use an ocean blue, flat container (Hawaii).

SUMMER:

(1) Angled bulrushes low across water, yellow dahlias in a water painting. Add a water-oriented accessory.

(2) One double-flowering hibiscus cut short, and a small cluster of dwarf bamboo. Arrange in coconut (remove meat). Set coconut shell on a napkin ring for balance. Makes an unusual centerpiece for a bridge-table dessert occasion (tropical).

(3) Oregon grape branches, thinned, and carnations in vertical style. Add a man-made rhythm material. Screening?

LATE SUMMER:

(1) Long, slender, hanging leaves of pampas grass and late-blooming iris (unusual combination).

(2) Cosmos and sumac. Mass sumac very short; cosmos tall. (Shock appeal, because of nature's reverse positioning.)

EARLY FALL:

(1) Branch with small apples (or any fruit) and zinnias. Vertical pattern in a tall vase.

(2) Sea fan and anemones in triple-stacked containers.

FALL:

(1) Bare branches with pomegranate fruit, white mums (Japan).

(2) Pampas plumes and red anthurium (Hawaii).

WINTER:

(1) Pyracantha berries, carnations, pine. (Substitute China root for pyracantha, temperate zone.)
(2) Magnolia, or winged euonymous (bare of leaves), two colors of roses, cream and red.
(3) Christmas: gilded lotus pods, red candle, holly cut short. Vertical pattern.

LATE WINTER:

(1) Quince branches in bloom, sculptured (Japan).
(2) Forsythia branches, brown lotus seedpods in background. Spring flowers, if available.

12

On-Table Arrangements

Time, effort, pleasure, and money go into the creation of flower arrangements. They should be seen and appreciated. Did you realize that most flower arrangements are put in places designed for other purposes? We make coffee-table arrangements, buffet-table arrangements, entry-hall arrangements, and so on. Rarely is there a place specifically for displaying flowers. We designate our arrangements by setting rather than by sight or designs. Let's shift our emphasis to the arrangement.

The freedom to place flowers anywhere is highly desirable. In the limited living quarters a new bride has, table space is frequently at a premium. To expand possibilities, consider areas off tables, such as walls, ceilings, doors, the floor.

With many settings available the challenge still remains: how will the arrangement look to a viewer? To answer the challenge, consciously consider sight lines or viewing angles.

The principle of sight lines doesn't discriminate between On-table and Off-table arrangements; it applies to both positionings. However, to make discussion rational, a division has been made between the two. This chapter deals with On-table viewing; the next with Off-table viewing. Through experience, the following classifications have proved helpful, workable, uncomplicated:

(1) One-view, or front-viewing styles, with sight lines coming from only one angle
(2) Two-sided views: sight lines come from two angles,
    (a) front-back style
    (b) front-adjacent-side style
(3) Three-sided view
(4) All-around view: the centerpiece

Viewing Angles: One and Two

A one-viewing arrangement has sight lines coming from just one view, usually the front. Sight lines could come from the top, also. Isn't it hard for a reader to imagine a pictured arrangement as anything but one view? The Vertical and Cascading patterns make eye-arresting one-views. Try either for first efforts.

The two-view style is divided into two parts. The first is front-back setting, opposing sides on view. Immediately the dining table and a tête-à-tête supper for two come to mind, where the wide V-shape pattern would be perfect. Can you imagine it as a pretty frame for you?

A suggestion: when you try the wide-angled V, use a combination rather than only flower blooms. If your budget allows for half-a-dozen roses, buy three roses rather than splurging all at once, and use a Character element. For example, use three tall leaves; some green bulrushes; a little pine. Buy short-stemmed roses because the arrangement needs short flowers. Short stems are cheaper. Then, the next week, use the rest of your budget on three more fresh roses.

The two-view can also be used in a room-divider module. The open shelves of a room-divider module provide a fine spot for the Peacock pattern. Think about this fact: the Peacock pattern in the divider could act either as a blocking-of-the-view arrangement or as a "veiling" arrangement. (Check Plant Identification for suggestions, p. 200.)

The second part of the two-view style is the front-adjacent-side positioning. The style is useful in corners or entryways. Often entryways can be seen from the living room. Entryways and corners need the type of flower material that is beautiful close up and beautiful from a distance. This arranging problem is common for the other views too.

Where viewing is diverse, flower materials and containers need these pertinent values:

(1) Flower material attractive from two (or three) sides
(2) Flower material that has physical bulk, or
(3) Flower material that has visual weight
(4) Container with interest:
    (a) large, or
    (b) an objet d'art, or
    (c) combination of two or more vases

Plate 31
(p. 158)

The arrangement in plate 31 is designed for an entryway with the living area off to the left. As one comes in, the eye naturally travels along the line of driftwood, then is caught by the glitter of copper mesh, and, finally, the beautiful orchids—an impressive combination.

From the living-room area, the orchids are emphasized; the copper mesh is less obvious but still eye-catching because of its sparkle. The massed green leaves give a fresh feel against the beige driftwood, as well as complementing the orchid spray.

A black container, just visible by the driftwood's left leg, holds water to keep greens and orchids fresh. Blending into the arrangement from the living area, it's unnoticed from the entryway. Take a minute to check the arrangement against the criteria of pertinent values needed for the setting:

    Physical bulk: driftwood is 24 inches long; massed greens
    Visual weight: exotic orchids; shine of copper mesh
    Size: arrangement length, 30 inches; height, 18 inches; depth, 10 inches
    Container: ceramic. Also, driftwood acts as a container.

On-Table Arrangements 173

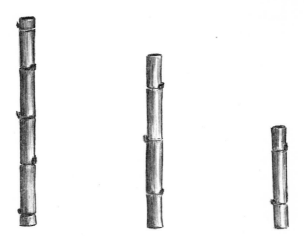

FIG. 44. Relative heights for bamboo.

The arrangement "feel" invites the viewer into the living area, an excellent arrangement for an entryway.

Two-view arrangements emphasizing height (driftwood emphasizes length) can give an important vertical feel to a low-ceilinged room. The most obvious way to achieve a soaring effect is with a tall vase and flowers placed in the Vertical pattern. However, consider flower material other than driftwood which can be used as bulk with perhaps little cost to you. Three ideas follow:

(1) Use three birch logs at least $2\frac{1}{2}$ inches in diameter. Have one cut 24 inches tall; one cut 20 inches; the last 12 inches. Use glycerinized fall foliage. No water is needed. Tack the branches to the logs.

(2) Select pieces of giant bamboo. Scale dimensions like those of birch logs. See figure 44. Drill holes 3 inches above any node with a hand drill. Enlarge to half an inch, then fill with water. Use small fresh flowers, cascading.

(3) Suspend one piece of bamboo in a vertical fashion. Add flowers from the top or drill a hole.

Bulk can be achieved by using bulky household utensils, or even machinery, as containers: an antique urn, a large brass or iron kettle, a coal scuttle. Secondhand shops or boutiques may yield plow discs.

Plow discs are large, heavy, plate-shaped metal circles with a hole in the center, formerly used on old-time plows. They are already popular with flower arrangers because of their shape and texture. Place one disc on top of the other but separate them by 3 or 4 inches with a pipe joint which can be found in any plumbing shop. They come in assorted sizes and are inexpensive. Make your arrangement in the top disc only. For fresh flowers, use a small tin can, painted black, to hold water.

Cover the bottom disc with pebbles leaving plenty of space between pebbles and the top disc. Pebbles give the impression of water without the fuss of actual water. No plow discs? How about large machinery-type gears, about 6 inches in diameter?

Three-View Style

A three-view is seen from the front and both sides, or from a side, front, and top. Can you think of other combinations? In any event, there is a back to the arrangement. A few of the many places for such a viewing situation include: table or chest against a wall, end table, book case, TV.

The three-view style can be used for a table decoration. The basic requirement is the background. Provide it by moving the dining table against a wall or curtain. For a sit-down affair, think of the possibilities for creativity. If the height of the table decoration need no longer be a controlling factor, the design field is expanded immeasurably.

Plate 29 (p. 156) The photograph (plate 29) shows a three-sided table decoration created for a seafood buffet party. Appropriate shell serving-dishes as well as individual shells with crab soufflé were used.

Sea shells can be used as containers. They can be grouped artistically on a table to be marveled at for their colorings and shapes. They also can be mounted on rods with bases and used as objets d'art. Silver some and use harmoniously with other silver accessories on a formal table.

The magnificant 26-inch ocean blue container holds white, bleached edgeworthia wired to a long stick placed inside the container. Parts of edgeworthia are wedged inside the container for firmer support. After locating the balance point of the shell, it was slipped in among the branches of edgeworthia. Pressure holds it upright.

The Centerpiece

The fourth and last viewing style is the all-around style, the centerpiece—four sides and the top.

Two traditional rules govern height and length of Western centerpieces for a sit-down meal. They have been time-tested, and it would be wise to heed them.

THE FIRST RULE: the maximum height of flower material and/or accessories for a centerpiece is placed at 18 inches. A centerpiece taller than 18 inches could limit table conversation; it is difficult to converse through intervening foliage or eye-level candlelight. Eighteen inches normally allow for easy viewing across a table, but after completing your table decoration check the sight lines yourself. Sit down at each place to learn how your guests will view not only the arrangement but each other.

Practical application? Try the Peacock pattern. Keep the height of the tallest fan-point at 18 inches. Measure this point to the table surface, not the container rim. If the fan is too high, be ruthless!

THE SECOND RULE: the length of a table decoration must include all accessories—the arrangement, candles, figures, and the like. The grouping should measure $\frac{1}{3}$ the length of the table surface. For example, if your table is 60 inches long, the table decoration will measure 20 inches; perhaps

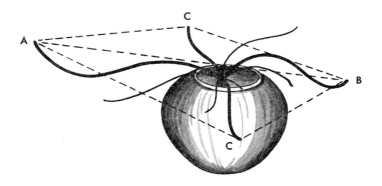

Fig. 45. Horizontal pattern, double-triangle design.

14 inches for flowers, 6 inches for candles. If your table is oval or round, the centerpiece grouping should measure $\frac{1}{3}$ of the diameter. However, when estimating the requisite length, consider realigning measurements into smaller components. It can work like this:

Assume you are planning a sit-down party for four people. The table measures 72 inches; by rule, the decoration will total 24 inches. So the flower arrangement (no accessories) can equal two 12-inch arrangements; three 8-inch arrangements; or four 6-inch arrangements. The four 6-inch ones may be individual arrangements at each place setting.

The grouping of two, three, or four separate arrangements can be neatly spaced through the table center; or they can be placed at each end. Or they can be made into an elongated S-shape down the middle, or put in an oval or circle style. Table corners could be a happy choice. So within the rule, wide variety is possible.

Any container, as long as it's less than 18 inches high, is a possibility for a centerpiece vase. Patterns for tall vases can always include the Cascading as well as Horizontal. With either pattern, fewer flowers are required than for a traditional massed arrangement. Fewer flowers are easier on the budget, easier to arrange. The sketches show some ideas (figs. 45–49).

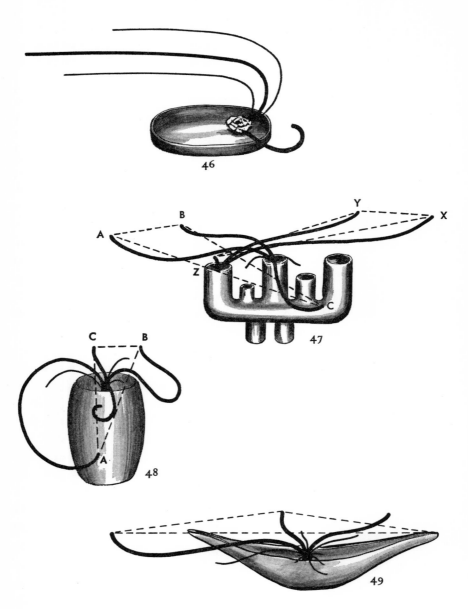

FIG. 46. Pattern for dry branches or sculptured roots.

FIG. 47. Horizontal pattern, centerpiece arrangement in a modern container.

FIG. 48. Centerpiece design for a small area. Deep curves accent the container.

FIG. 49. Horizontal pattern in a boat-shaped container. Peaks of the boat act as triangle points.

Exceptions are always possible to the rules on length and height for centerpieces, but keep in mind the basic reason for the rules: comfortable conversation in a beautiful, easily viewed setting.

Suppose an arrangement measures too small. You have a 20-inch arrangement to fill a 24-inch space. What can be done about it?

First of all, you can expand the arrangement by cutting a fresh A point, longer than the original; then add flower material to fill. Or put the arrangement on a 24-inch flat mat or wooden base, which immediately gives it more visual bulk. Another way—add an accessory: a pair of candle holders and candles, a figure, flat stones, a chunk of pretty glass.

If the question were asked, "What kind of flower arrangement do you need most frequently?" the answer would certainly be, "A centerpiece for the dining table." Your next thought: "Wish I could think of something a little different."

Most problems for a party setting arise because of a needed inspiration for a centerpiece. Usually ideas are sparked by immediate or imminent happenings: a special season of the year (Christmas, Thanksgiving), a birthday, a celebration, a shower, a promotion. Sometimes small things inspire us, such as seeing fresh tulips in a store window. Mostly, though, a conscious effort must be made to get an idea.

How about finding something in the marketplace while shopping for groceries? Why not an exceptionally beautiful Turban squash used for a flower container? Choose a large one that "sits" well. Slice off the top, hollow it out as you would for a jack-o-lantern. Cut intermittent holes around the body not too close to the base. Wedge short, dry, colorful autumn foliage through the holes.

Or just hollow out a pumpkin or squash and use it as a regular container with a pin cupholder in the bottom. Use alder branches with their wine-red catkins and pale lavender pompom dahlias; or cedar sprigs and Queen Anne's lace, an unusual combination against an orange pumpkin.

No squash or pumpkin? Substitute a fruit (watermelon?), another vegetable, or a gourd. The hollowed-out gourd in the photograph (plate 32) is a special kind from Japan. It has been lacquered both inside and out, but the natural pattern of the skin is obvious. The shape is unusually attractive. Notice the minimum of flower material. Yet each piece is highlighted, and the arrangement doesn't appear thin.

Plate 32
(p. 159)

Applying the concept of creativity—new handling of familiar ideas—let's take a look at centerpieces that use no water, no container, no pinholders.

A common example is the arrangement used to celebrate a bountiful harvest. Giving thanks for good crops is universal; each country has fruits and vegetables attractively displayed on tables. In the Western world, Thanksgiving bounty is arranged in baskets or trays, but often just laid on the table.

Likewise, there is a universal practice of decorating banquet tables for large gatherings with flowers and greens laid on tables. To the idea of flowers or food placed directly on a table, let's add one more ingredient: the three-dimensional quality of Ikebana. The result? Table paintings.

Table paintings have many of the same advantages as the *ukibana*:

(1) effectiveness in small areas
(2) minimum use of flower material
(3) effectiveness for "close-up" viewing
(4) impromptu assembly
(5) little or no need for equipment

What do you need? One important piece of flower material. Since water is unnecessary, this material may be dry. Good—it can be planned ahead and kept in storage until the moment it's wanted.

Requirements? First, the flower material must be large

enough and interesting enough to act as an attention-getter. The second criterion is that it must have three-dimensional potential.

Experience has proved to me it's easier to find a good 3-D piece than it is to create one from two or more materials. Perhaps you must learn this for yourself. An obvious choice is driftwood, but a 3-D branch is usually more available.

A three-dimensional branch would be one that has three points that can rest firmly on the table and yet allow noticeable space underneath. Clearing the table by 1 to 3 inches is plenty. Check the list of foliage for sculpturing on page 65. With these you can avoid the pitfall of a long length of straight branch lying flat on the table.

A good branch, once selected and sculptured, can be used with a minimum of its foliage for a first arrangement. See *Plate 33* plate 33. Use as bare branches with flowers or berries *(p. 159)* the next time. Perhaps spray paint it a third time.

Other possible 3-D materials could be roots, coral formations of branching types, well-chosen branches of glycerinized fall foliage that could be gently interwined for the 3-D effect.

The root category deserves special attention. The use of living roots in a flower arrangement may seem strange to you, but don't dismiss the idea casually. Centuries ago, the Japanese used exposed roots in arrangements called *morimono*. *Morimono* have a special charm, so let's borrow some of the ideas.

All roots of the plant to be used must be meticulously washed, air-dried, then carefully displayed in their gleaming whiteness or brownness. Root materials for table paintings should be used shortly after cleaning. However, the plants can be kept in pots until the day before you need them. After use, repot. They will continue growing.

What root specimens are best? Attractive ones include the ground-orchid root system *(Cymbidium virescens)* and the white fleshy root system of the spider-grass plant, a very common garden specimen available inexpensively at your

FIG. 50. Spider-grass plant with cleaned roots.

local nursery (fig. 50). The third suggestion is the *Rhodea japonica* with its white roots. A gardener neighbor might give you more ideas.

Flowers that hold well out of water and those that have a capability to sit squarely with their stems cut off are useful for table paintings. Fulfilling both conditions are carnations, dahlias, camellias, orchids, daisies, chrysanthemums, and pinks. Condition them well before cutting heads off the stems. Like water paintings, table paintings may need needlepoint holders.

For your first attempt, hide a pinholder among the roots of spider grass. Arrange flowers of the long-stemmed freesia among the grass blades, using about seven. Put arrangement on a roofing-tile.

A technical problem arises with a table-painting arrangement. A table painting approximates in height many items used on a dining table: serving dishes, plates, cups, glasses. Competition for attention is keen.

Delineating the area covered by the table painting helps to set it apart. Again, borrowing from the Japanese *morimono* tradition, use a large leaf, palm fibers, tree bark, a broken handmade roofing tile, a flat basket, a wooden slab or burl, a cheese tray.

Bark from birch trees and palm fibers have both been tried for special outdoor parties. Before using, they were neatly cleaned, washed, and dried. Other "delineators," such as the tile or slab, not only set the arrangement apart but have the added advantage of raising it a couple of inches from the table surface.

Plate 25
(p. 152) In plate 25, the white, bleached, glycerinized fern sets off the arrangement nicely. The 3-D effect is achieved by intertwining stems of the woodroses. Since it is difficult to show three dimensions in a photograph, two pictures were taken of this centerpiece. If you study them closely, you will see how 3-D is acquired.

Plate 26
(p. 153) The second picture (plate 26) shows how the stems and heads of the woodroses have been gently interlaced to create depth. Notice how the flowers are veiled by the woodroses. The arrangement measures 24 inches long, 18 inches wide, 9 inches in depth. Most of the materials are dry and can be arranged many days in advance of the time they are to be used. Only the big white mums were put into the arrangement at the last moment.

Dry bulbs are wonderful materials to use in table paintings. They come in beautifully muted shades. Gladioli bulbs, in particular, have a nice spectrum of colors. Other bulbs attractive to use are hyacinths, lily, tulip, and narcissi.

A table-painting combination created for a class in flower arranging and thoroughly enjoyed was gladioli bulbs, matching fresh gladioli of the same species, and two bumble bees on flexible wires. The bees gave the whole arrangement a lilting, happy, whimsical feeling! We used a small cup pinholder to support the glads; the flowers were cut short. Added for contrast and to mask the pinholder were small sprays of asparagus greens.

Red potatoes and onions have long been popular for vegetable arrangements. Choose them next time with attached roots.

Besides a cup pinholder, several other mechanical aids come in handy for table paintings: lightweight wire to hold interlaced branches and double-backed cellophane tape to hold a piece of fruit in the right place or to fasten a curled leaf just so.

Pins can fasten extra berries, seedpods, or small fruit to strategic spots of branches if they have fallen off or have never grown there. Push two straight pins through a fruit, one from each side as you hold it to the twig. Cut off the protruding pin ends with flower scissors or wire cutters.

Avoid the following pitfalls when arranging a table painting:

(1) piled up greens and/or flowers that are all held together with wire
(2) an arrangement that looks too laborious—it should be light, airy, rhythmic, fun
(3) too many varieties of materials
(4) too short-lived materials (droopy flowers or greens are depressing)
(5) materials all in the same shape
(6) materials all of the same texture

13

Off-Table Arrangements

Off-table arrangements are suggested because they are such a boon for those in small quarters. An instant change to Off-table positioning can be merely a matter of repositioning. Instead of a table centerpiece, put a large flower arrangement on a pedestal or plant stand.

Pedestals are used for sculptures or for works of art traditionally, but they are suitable bases for flowers. Look in swap-and-shop areas; it's worth the time. Heights of pedestals vary, but 30 inches is useful for a flower arrangement because the average dining table is 30 inches high (fig. 51, p. 186). So if space on the dining table is limited, put an arrangement on a pedestal nearby. Use candles on the table. Check viewing angles from a sitting position for your "centerpiece." *Note:* Bulk with beauty should be your guide.

Sometimes older dwellings have wall sconces. If so, they are ready-made Off-table containers for you. Wire, Oasis, and flower material can quickly convert them into temporary Off-table arrangements.

For convenience, Off-table arrangements are divided into arrangements in or out of containers. In-container arrangements use ready-made containers attached directly to the wall or suspended from a ceiling moulding. If suspended, the container could hang free or rest lightly against the wall or screen. Use the patterns already discussed.

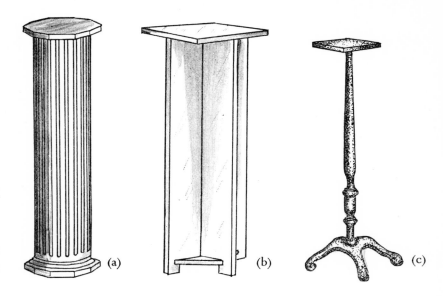

FIG. 51. Three types of pedestals: (a) wood; (b) lucite; (c) wrought iron.

Off-table arrangements can also be created from flower material as self-contained units, out-of-container arrangements. Such creations are flower sculptures. Often they are complete in themselves; more often they have flower material added.

Wall-hung Creations

Reference has already been made to several ideas for making arrangements in containers that are hung on walls. Most effective is to select one or two outstanding materials, then highlight them in space. Use beauty without bulk in this positioning. If you like the arrangement particularly, spotlight it.

For a buffet party, if you have room to put a narrow vertical arrangement on the table, combine it with a wall-hung arrangement. Harmonizing two flower compositions is attention-getting. One practice arranging-session a week ahead might forestall unforeseen problems.

FIG. 52. Wicker sculpture in natural beige color.

Flower sculptures are a fascinating field for creativity. Beginners, preferably, should use lightweight materials. Hobby and craft shops carry large assortments of dry materials: cording, raffia, rattan. Recheck the list of abstract and man-made materials on page 39. Flower materials for sculptures must have certain characteristics. They must be pliable; they should look beautiful fresh; they should look beautiful dried. Common ones available are: grape vines, bittersweet, corkscrew willow, thin rattan.

Particularly appealing to me is thin wicker. Wicker is not only pliable, it's also soft so it won't mar walls. It's pretty in its natural beige color, but is capable of taking many spray coats of paint, and keeps indefinitely.

In about 20 minutes, the sketched wall hanging was looped and tied with invisible wire (fig. 52). A small hook was wired to the wicker in back; a small picture hook on the wall was used to hang it. And there it was, a flower sculpture ready for flowers if I wished.

Plate 34
(p. 160)

Flowers are put into sculptures last. For the wicker sculpture, no water was required since I planned on flowers only for an evening. However, Oasis wrapped in foil could be fastened to a sculpture. (Water is heavy; allow for its weight.) In the picture (plate 34) no holding device was required; flowers and foliage were merely tucked in.

My favorite definition of design is "that which brings orderly form out of chaos." To insure orderly form rather than chaos, keep your initial efforts in flower sculpture to basic designs. Use two intertwining circles or ovals, or two intertwining triangles. Remember to check the size of the sculpture against its final positioning while you are creating.

Ceiling-hung Mobiles

Space problems for flower arrangements can be partially solved with ceiling-hung mobiles. Using mobiles over a dining table is not a new idea, but is infrequently tried.

For a sit-down dinner, mobiles do pose sight-line problems; for standing buffets, no problem. Mobiles are the solution for large parties in small spaces.

The biggest question for you is whether or not the end product will justify the time, effort, and possibly money expended. In short, how much value will you receive from a hand-made unit? The term value is a relative one chosen deliberately to make you aware of what you really want. A flower mobile or flower sculpture created by you is unique. How desirable is this achievement?

Suggestions follow for two simple mobiles. Both can hold flowers, or each is complete by itself. Both have the advantage of being capable of use and reuse. If the color bores you, one, at least, takes spray paint beautifully. Both are wonderful for emergencies; they are long-lasting.

The first is a mobile designed for Christmas, made out of tumbleweed. Tumbleweeds have interesting forms if you stop to examine them and overlook their nuisance angle. Where they grow, they grow in abundance!

FIG. 53. Pussy-willow mobile.

Find one that pleases you for its outline. Eliminate twigs
from the inside first. Then trim the perimeter. Remember
the "veiling" technique of 3-D. While shaping it, keep
checking the form. Would it look better upside down?
Try it. How about sideways? Try it.

After "sculpting," attach to the top, with wire, a swivel
fixture from a fishing-tackle box. Hang it on the clothesline
and spray it glossy white—three coats, not all at once but
one at a time. When dry, complete it with red cranberries
on the inside tip ends. It's lightweight, easy to handle, colorful. Hang with nylon thread.

To vary, suspend a tiny tin can under the swivel piece.
Put four holes (with a nail) near the rim of the tin can and
hang with nylon thread or nylon fish line. Place Oasis in
the can. Wire some bachelor's buttons internally, then cascade them down from the water-filled can. Or spray-paint
the mobile blue and cascade white flowers.

The second idea is to use fresh pussy willows. Form them
into two intersecting circles (or ovals); figure 53 shows

the unit. Use two pussy willows for each circle; tie inconspicuously at the top. Four tips are used as helpers. For the base, use Styrofoam, concealing it with fresh flower material. After bending, the pussy willows will not require water. They retain their fresh-looking charm for at least a month. Even when dried there is scarcely a noticeable change.

If you like the idea of Off-table arrangements, set up a fairly permanent wall fixture. Plan the hook for multi-purposes: pictures, pieces of driftwood, tapestry hangings, flower sculptures, or mobiles.

A little forethought can overcome problems in positioning. Take into consideration whether what you plan to hang is to be three-dimensional. If so, it will need extra space behind it; the hook may have to jut from the wall or moulding. Otherwise, any picture hook, lighting unit, wire, or chain assembly may serve the purpose. If you plan on hanging a mobile from a light fixture, check it first for weight-holding capabilities. Never guess. Check ceilings too before attaching any fixtures.

Door and Floor Pieces

There is no reason why door arrangements should be limited to holidays. Why only Christmas? Be an extra gracious hostess by hanging a basket of flowers on your screen door in October as well as in May—a nice way to great your friendly neighbor. Need an idea?

An old wicker purse large enough to accommodate an orange-juice can will do nicely. Spray-paint the purse with a thick coat of white or orange. Put a small screw eye, or loop a paper-covered wire, through the wicker at the back and attach to the door. Fill the can with water and add pinks, glycerinized fall foliage, or begonias. Berries last a long time. Veil the wicker with airy fern to give it a more gentle look.

If you are thinking of door arrangements, stretch your

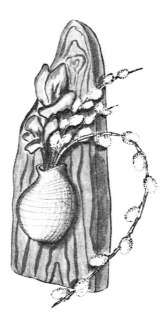

Fig. 54. Two gladioli and three pussy-willow tips in a thin ceramic container attached to a 3-foot grained board.

imagination beyond the door itself to include the door frame. Removing an interior door and using the frame side for a hanging arrangement would be a refreshing change. *Plate 3* shows a hanging arrangement as does figure 54. The sketch shows one Japanese way. With a slender branch and a few flowers, a small beauty spot is created where none was before.

Plate 3 *(p. 44)*

When considering floor arrangements, space might prove as big a problem as with On-table arrangements. But, if not, a floor-arrangement happening is much fun.

Floor sculptures are advanced Ikebana, but I have watched beginners help assemble floor arrangements as a "team" effort with great delight. Some preparation by a hostess is, of course, necessary. She provides container and flower materials. However, you can complete one with two or three friends before a party. Use adjoining walls for a background but keep the arrangement a foot away from the wall.

Off-Table Arrangements 191

FLOWER MATERIAL: Three heavy branches about the thickness of your forearm are the minimum and most important requirement. Choose them so that they will go together into a three-footed structure. Three points will form a firm basis for a sculpture. Obtain the branches several days ahead of time so that you can study them and think out the best way to nail them together. Remove all the foliage unless you are using pine.

Besides the structural branches, you'll need small-leaved branches for foliage, five to seven large flowers, and perhaps some asparagus or fern. Mock orange, privet, and loquat have long-lasting foliage.

TOOLS: a saw, wire, garden clippers, hammer, nails, and two tin cans spray-painted black with two *kenzan* to fit. Clay in the *kenzan* and wire the tin cans to the back of your structural branches to hold water for the fresh flower materials.

METHOD OF WORK: One person holds the branches; one person wires or nails; the third person critiques the positioning of material.

SUGGESTIONS ON MATERIALS for a structure: white birch, giant bamboo, scorched timbers, rail fencing, red sugarcane, rattan stalks.

Concluding the floor-arrangement ideas are two unusual suggestions. Read them both before you say they are impossible. The first is inspired by the ancient Chinese art of "table culture."

Table culture, which has now evolved into the modern *bonsai,* was the art of making potted plants into pleasing landscapes. The two arts, plant table culture and table flower arranging, thrived side by side in ancient China. Why not incorporate these two ancient arts into your own lifestyle?

Acquire (purchase or grow) any variety of beautiful, interestingly shaped plant, large in size (at least 3 feet). Two basic requirements:

(1) The plant should have small leaves.

(2) The plant should have an intricate branching system.

It is necessary to point out that the effectiveness of the arrangement depends on the beauty of the plant and the restraint of the arranger.

Put the plant on a pedestal in a well-chosen spot. Of course, it will be beautiful as is. However, when the occasion demands, fasten to or weave through the branches colorful ripe berries: pyracantha, cotoneaster, snowberries, winterberries, etc. Do not remove the berries from their stems, but do remove leaves.

Be careful to set berries in their living manner so they are not hung from the plant as if they were Christmas-tree ornaments. Don't overburden. Small fruits or seedpods can be substituted. Use lady apples, quince, chestnut burrs, or star apples attached invisibly to branches of the plant by thin wire.

After the fruit or berries are fixed, select two or at most three flowers and arrange carefully. These must be special flowers: peonies, magnolias, climbing roses, hibiscus, camellias. In short, the flowers must be tree-growing. Use no ground-growers or garden-type flowers: no carnations, no zinnias, no mums. Thus, you will achieve a feeling of Ikebana, as well as the spirit of old China.

To keep flowers fresh, use tiny balloons filled with water, or the orchid tubes mentioned in the chapter on equipment (p. 125). The berries, if properly conditioned, will last a long time without water.

The second idea is the same general plan. Instead of a plant, choose large weathered driftwood. Anchor it securely with rocks in a large container and arrange the berries or flowers through it for special occasions.

In general, Off-table arrangements take a little more time to prepare than do On-table ones. But, if you are a person who enjoys being different, Off-table flower sculptures and arrangements are a fertile field.

14

Your Flower-Arranging Future

When you are considering future plans for a home, remember flower arranging. When you go house-hunting, look over new homes for the special flower-arranging areas now built into many.

These areas have storage cabinets for equipment, for containers, driftwood, etc. They have a sink for cleaning materials and a table for arranging. These are wonderful assets, particularly the storage units.

If the choice is possible, think carefully about a space to display your arrangements rather than only a place to arrange them. Flower arranging is best done where the arrangement is to be viewed. It's easier to achieve visual proportion, easier to get the "feel" of how the design will look, if the arrangement is made where it is to be shown.

Important too, there is less likely to be a disaster en route! Flower arrangements are heavy sometimes. Think about putting the emphasis on viewing, rather than making.

Remember, Character arrangements are flower materials as a form of living beauty. Relate them to yourself.

The SKIN: The design and plan of the arrangement.

The FLESH: Flower material and container.

The BONE: The inner, unseen support: technique.

The SOUL: An intangible feeling, or essence, both of the creator and the flower material. Combined, they make beautiful harmony.

Appendices

1. *Attributes of Fresh Leaves*

TEXTURE	Shiny	Matte	Rough
	carissa	narcissus	begonias
	holly	eucalyptus	lantana
	magnolia	sea grape	loquat

COLOR	Yellow-Green		Dark-Green
	golden euonymous		hawthorn
	bamboo		yew
	philodendron family		pittosporum
	Red		Coppery
	Japanese red plum		copper beech
	rhubarb		castor bean (new leave

SHAPE	Needle	Sword	Ovate
	asparagus	gladiolus	camellia
	pine	New Zealand flax	azalea
	podocarpus	lauhala	prickly pear cactus
		dracaena	

SIZE	Small		Medium
	spiraea		magnolia
	nandina		camellia
	azalea		oak
	liriope (grass-like)		

FRAGRANCE	Spicy and Sweet
	lemon myrtle, boxwood, many evergreens, citrus trees, acerola cherry,

ROOTING	ivy, privet, pussy willow, all willows, cane grass, sansevieria, gardenia,

DURABILITY	Cut Branches
	gumwood, rubber tree, camellia, azalea, holly, loquat, cryptomeria,

MOISTURE	No water needed:
	cactus, sansevieria, monstera, pineapple leaves, agave, many succulent

Ribbed	Quilted	Hairy	Velvety
canna aspidistra fan palm	hosta alocasia	African violet	dusty miller kalanchoe

Blue-Green		Gray-Green	
spruce blue gumwood		olive agave many cacti	

Silvery	Variegated	Special
artemisia silver tree silver acacia	"gold-dust" leaves flowering kale begonias	autumn foliage croton, caladium, and other tropicals

Palmate/Lobed	Feathery	Fan	Serrated Edge
maple aralia common fig	ferns acacia	palm ginkgo	loquat hydrangea mahonia oak

Large	Very Large
palmetto aspidistra philodendron family	monstera banana palms

most eucalyptus, spice tree

geraniums, tillandsia

	Single Leaf
magnolia, pine	monstera, aspidistra, bamboo palm, ti leaf, succulents

rosettes, such as echeveria, aeonium varieties

2. Relating Flower Materials to Container

	CONTAINERS (Basic Characteristics)		CHARACTERISTIC
SHAPE	Circle and oval: plate types, bottle shapes, some footed compotes		Round: Oval: Cone:
	Fan		Fan:
	Rectangle and triangle		Triangle: Arrow: Sword:
TEXTURE	Smooth: metals, glossy ceramics, glass		Shiny:
	Matte: bisque-finish ceramics, dull metals, frosted glass		Dull:
	Rough: modern ceramics, iron, some wooden containers, bark, driftwood		Rough:
COLOR	Any color container, including white and black (See color diagram.)		Monochromatic: tints Analogous: adjacent
DESIGN MOTIFS	Natural		Identical to motif:
	Linear: horizontal, vertical		Linear, placed hori-
	Abstract		Man-made: copper

FLOWER MATERIAL	
IN HARMONY	IN CONTRAST
carnations, dahlias, dollar eucalyptus, sea-grape leaves, mums, daisies	delphinium, liatris, spiraea, orchid sprays, pandanus leaves, ti leaves, pine branches, forsythia branches
hyacinth, rose, azalea leaves pine cones, calla lilies	
tulips, gingko leaves	hydrangeas, peonies, alliums, monstera leaves (round)
bird of paradise, iris anthurium and alocasia leaves New Zealand flax	Mass materials in circular forms.
anthurium, capsicum berries, holly leaves, camellia leaves	driftwood, pussy willow (furry), pampas grass, artichoke seedpods (spiky)
celosia (velvety), roses, some rocks and pebbles, aloe leaves, sage	holly berries, aspidistra leaves, bamboo stalks and leaves
yarrow, statice, scotch broom, some seed-pods, rocks, Styrofoam balls, cattails	bleached wistaria, ferns (feathery), plumosa fern (lacy), plastic rain (very shiny)
and shades of a basic color	Opposites: blue container, yellow flower material
colors on color diagram	Near contrast: apricot-colored container, flower material in lavenders
pine with pine	
zontally(or vertical ly):edgeworthia, bulrushes, scotch broom	Ball shapes, or massed greens or flowers. Also linear materials such as cattails—vertical for horizontal vase; horizontal for vertical vase
wire, glass marbles, etc. used with flowers	Contrasting abstract elements: plastic with glass, etc.

3. *Plant Identification*

The following pages contain a listing of many of the plants that are suitable for flower arranging. The common name is on the left, followed by the botanical terms and other common names, if any. Valuable information about the appearance and use of the plant is also included for many of the entries. Each species of a family varies, so the reader who cannot locate one of the plants in a particular flower store is advised to inquire about another variety. Also, please note that terminology and spelling differ slightly according to the authority consulted. Cross-references are given.

acacia—*Acacia baileyana* F. Mueller; mimosa. Keep out of drafts for longer life of the fluffy flowers.

acerola cherry—(1) *Malpighia punicifolia* L. Cherry-size scarlet fruit on evergreen branches, edible. Unusual spicy fragrance to crushed leaves. (2) *M. glabra;* Barbados cherry. Smaller fruit, not quite so attractive.

aeonium—*A. arboreum atropurpuremem.* A succulent with dark purple rosettes; long-lasting. Check other varieties of aeoniums for interesting color.

African daisy—*see* gerbera daisy.

agapanthus—*Agapanthus umbellatus* L'Her; blue lily, lily of the Nile. Flower and stem are both beautiful; a white variety is also available.

agave—*A. agave americana;* century plant.

airplane plant—*see* spider plant.

alder—*Alnus japonica.* Useful especially when branches have cones, either green or dried.

alliums—Some members of the onion family have clustered ornamental flowers above contorted stems; good for line arranging. Best species for arrangements is *Allium albopilosum.*

alocasia—(1) *Alocasia sanderiana*. A beautiful, large, heavily-veined leaf; arrow-shaped; comes in shades of green or variegated; (2) *A. cucullata;* Chinese taro. Heart-shaped leaf is less durable, but more easily available, and cheaper.

amaryllis—(1) *Hippeastrum hybridum* Hort. (2) *H. Amaryllis belladonna;* belladonna lily.

ananas—*Ananas comosus* Ruby. Ornamental pineapple with narrow green or red leaves, red flowers, and small red pineapples.

anemone—*Anemone japonica;* windflower. A common flower with pretty shape and color.

anthurium—*Anthurium andreanum* Lind. Cultivated for both leaves and flowers; many varieties available. Investigate the so-called *obake* (ghost anthurium) with white, pink, or green markings.

apple—*Malus pumila* Mill. var. *dulcissima* Koidz. Use branches with fruit or when in flower. *See also* crabapple.

apricot—*Prunus armeniaca* var. *Ansu maxim.* Flowers come before leaves. Cut branch while in bud; leaves will appear several days after buds unfold. Branches can be enjoyed for two or more weeks.

aralia—*Aralia cordata* Thunb. *See also* fatsia.

arbor vitae—*Thuja orientalis* L. Use like cedar.

areca—*Areca catechu* L.; betel-nut palm. Fronds are airy and very pretty in arrangements; fruit, yellow to orange.

arnotto—*Bixa orellana* L.; "lipstick" plant or dye plant. Seedpods are ornamental, both fresh and dried; available in Hawaii and the Philippines.

artemisia—*Artemisia albula;* silver king. Family of sagebrush. Silvery foliage is ornamental.

artichoke—(1) *Cynara scolymus* L. Has a purple flower; thistle-like; leaves are gray-green, velvety; submerge them for conditioning; (2) *C. cardunculus.* Dried seedpod, the choke, is usually called cardone puff in flower shops. Natural color is beige; it may be dyed all colors.

arum lily—*Zantedeschia aethiopica* Spreng.; calla lily. Leaf, flower, and stem are all attractive. Score the stem with a fork before conditioning for better water intake.

ash—(1) *Rosaceae sorbus americana;* mountain ash. The clusters of orange-red berries are beautiful; (2) *R. sorbus aucuparia;* rowan tree; (3) *R. sorbus commixta.* Autumn-tinted foliage extra lovely.

asparagus—(1) *Asparagus cochinchinensis* Merr.; bamboo asparagus, large needles; (2) *Asparagus sprengeri.* Bright green needles that last all year. Mature plants have fragrant, pinkish flowers that turn into red berries. Excellent potted plant if well fertilized every two weeks; (3) *Asparagus plumosus* Baker; plumosa fern. Florists often use individual fronds. Grows like a vine; good for cascading style; (4) *A. racemosus* Wild.; thorny-type, climbing asparagus. Try small cuttings in *morimono*.

aspidistra—*Aspidistra elatior* Blume. Dark green leaf; also a variety banded in white or with white streaks. Unusually hardy. Grow in pots.

aster—*Aster savatieri*. Spring variety.

aucuba—*Aucuba japonica* Thunb.; variegated laurel, sometimes called gold-dust leaf. *See also* laurel. Aucuba can be glycerinized.

azalea—*Rhododendron obtusum* Planch. Large family; all colors.

baby's breath—(1) *Gypsophila paniculata* L. Excellent fresh and dried; (2) *Gypsophila;* Bristol fairy. New variety; flowers slightly larger.

baby woodrose—*see* woodrose.

bachelor's button—*C. cyanus* L.; cornflower.

bamboo—(1) *Phyllostachys reticulata* C. Koch; giant timber bamboo. Has strong runners; common. (2) *Sasa veitchii* Rehd.; striped bamboo. Very pretty, low-growing, strong-running bamboo with broad leaves. Develops straw-colored edges in summer and fall.

bamboo asparagus—*see* asparagus.

bamboo orchid—*Arundina bambusifolia* Lindl. Beautiful leaves; small purple flower. Common in Hawaii and Philippines. Easy to grow. Use in Peacock pattern.

bamboo palm—*see* hemp palm.

bamboo roots—*Phyllostachys aurea,* for example. Choose any of the running, not clump, varieties of bamboo. Dig up runners for use in arranging.

bamboo shoots—Tender, two- to three-foot new sprouts of any bamboo. They resemble long, thin, brown tubers with perhaps a green tip. Shoots are good eating, good arranging.

banana flower—*Musa coccinea,* also called *musa rubra*. Ornamental banana blossom, orange.

banana heart—*Musa sapientum* L. var. *Compressa*. Common purple flower.

Barbados cherry—*See* acerola.

beech—*Fagaceae fagus grandifolia*. One of the loveliest of the beeches.

begonia—*Begoniaceae* family is very large. Investigate tuberous begonias and *Begonia rex* Putz.

bells of Ireland—*Moluccella laevis* L.; molucca balm, also sometimes called shell flower. Annual herb with greenish calyx, bell-shaped. Dries well.

betel-nut palm—*see* areca.

birch—*Betula papyrifera* Marsh; white birch, paper-bark birch.

bird of paradise—(1) *Strelitzia reginae* Banks. Familiar orange and blue tropical flower. Long stem and leaf are both attractive; (2) *Strelitzia nicolai* Regel. Steel gray-blue and white, very large flower, stem very short. Usually two or three heads on one short stem.

bird's nest fern—*Asplenium nidus* L. An air plant needing warm weather, plenty of moisture. In proper climate, grows quickly and profusely. Long green leaf with wavy edges.

bittersweet—(1) *Solanum dulcamara;* woody nightshade. A climbing vine with yellow berries in fall which pop open to reveal a brilliant orange seed in each center. Dries in good condition; (2) *Celastrus scandens;* false bittersweet, celastrus. Same characteristics but smaller.

blackberry lily—*Belamcanda chinensis,* L. DC.; leopard lily or fan lily. A spotted orange, small flower that stands over fan-shaped, iris-like leaves. Easy to grow; very satisfying plant for Ikebana. Seedpods and leaves are also good for arranging.

black-eyed Susan—*see* daisy.

blue lily—*see* agapanthus.

Boston fern—*Nephrelepis cordifolia.* Very common, sword-type fern.

bougainvillea—*Bougainvillea spectabilis.* Common, purplish-red. Many colors and shadings in family. Remove leaves before conditioning.

box, boxwood—(1) *Buxus sempervirens.* An evergreen shrub with small glossy leaves; (2) *B. S. suffrutecosa.* A dwarf variety.

bridal wreath—(1) *Spiraea prunifolia plena.* A good spiraea for cutting; (2) *S. cantoniensis* Lour. Flat, double flowers on arching branches. Check other spiraea varieties.

broom—(1) *Cytisus scoparius* Link. Scotch broom is best known for its slender, pliable stalks; (2) *Thysanolaena maxima* Roxb.; tambo broom or tiger grass from the Philippines. Varying shades of color give the dry grass a most distinctive look. *See also* genista.

buckwheat—*Eriogonum giganteum;* St. Catherine's lace. Dried, lacy clusters on slender stems are both durable and attractive. Pick before flowers begin to shatter.

bulrush—*Scirpus californicus.* Three-angled, long, unbranched, spongy stem of dark green. Grows to 9 feet tall.

bunny tail—*Lagurus ovatus,* S. A.; hare's tail grass in Australia. *See also* foxtail.

cactus—(1) *C. hylocereus undatus;* night-blooming cereus. Chosen not for its unusual flowers, which last only a few hours, but for its interesting, fleshy, jointed, three-winged stems. Very thorny; (2) barrel cactus. Small ones are fun to work with; (3) the *Opuntia* family; the prickly pear cactus. Two or three of the pale green joints are wonderful with red roses in flower arrangements.

caladium—*Caladium bicolor* Vent.; common caladium. Grow in flower pots.

calendula—*Calendula officinalis* L.; also pot marigold.

calla lily—*see* arum lily.

camellia—(1) *Camellia japonica.* A single-petalled flower; (2) *Camellia sasanqua* Thunb. Camellias take three weeks to glycerinize; leaves turn a deep brown. Fresh camellia leaves are very long-lasting. An extremely beautiful family.

cane grass—*see* reed, giant.

canna—*Canna indica* L. Short-lived flower; leaves are durable; plant easy to grow; wide variety of colors.

capsicum—*Capsicum annum* L.; pepper plant. Fruits range in different varieties from cherry-shaped to conical; vari-colored.

cardone puff—*see* artichoke.

carissa—*Carissa grandiflora* A. DC.; De Candolle; natal plum. Star-like white, fragrant flowers; bright red, oval fruit; long-lasting foliage, sharp thorns. Excellent for flower arranging.

carnation—*Dianthus caryophyllus* L. Rich, clove-like fragrance. Wide selection possible; *see also* pink, sweet william, dianthus.

castor bean—*Ricinus communis;* castor oil plant. Unusually shaped leaf; the red-stemmed is more attractive than the white-stemmed. Stalks, seed capsules, leaves are all usable. Plant is poisonous; may produce allergy reactions. Handle carefully.

cattail—*Typa latifolia* L.; reed mace.

caustiz—swamp grass. Can be curled and glycerinized; lacy, very lovely. Preserved color, very dark brown; takes spray paint well in glycerinized state.

cedar—*see* cryptomeria.

celastrus—*see* bittersweet.

celosia—*Celosia cristata* L.; cockscomb, comb-style. There is also a plume variety of celosia. Glycerinize to keep.

"cereal puff"—*see* Philippine seedpods.

cherry—*Prunus serrulata* Lindl.; Japanese flowering cherry.

chestnut—*Castanea dentata*. Keep spiky seedpods on long stems when arranging.

China root—*Smilax china*. Pretty red berries; long lasting.

Chinese bellflower—*Platycodon grandiflorum*. Lovely blue color.

Chinese lantern—*Physalis alkekengi;* Japanese lantern. Orange seedpods in puff lantern shape; produced in fall.

Christmas rose—*Heleborus niger* L. Lovely single flower, white. Dark green, slender leaf. Carefully condition material for arranging with a small pin, like the morning glory.

chrysanthemum—the family is large; hundreds of types.

clivia—*Clivia miniata* Regel; Kafir lily. A brilliant orange cluster.

club moss—*see* lycopodium.

cockscomb—*see* celosia.

coffee-berry sprays—*R. coffea arabica*. Easy to grow in warm climates. Time is needed to produce berries on branches. Prone to many bugs. Berries grow close to stem; there are always several stages of ripening berries from green to yellow to red on each branch.

coleus—*Coleus blumei* Benth. Plant grown for its ornamental foliage. Will root in water, but droops until roots begin; therefore, cut stalk two or three weeks before using.

copper beech—*F. silvatica atropunicea*. Beech has beautiful branching habits and color.

corkscrew willow—*see* willow.

cornflower—*Centaurea cyanus* L.; bachelor's button.

cornplant—*Dracaena sanderiana* Sander; striped cornplant.

cosmos—*Cosmos bipinnatus* Cav. Very common.

cotoneaster—(1) *Cotoneaster horizontalis;* rock cotoneaster (2) *C. pannosa* Franch. Variety used in Hawaii.

crabapple—*Malus micromalus* Makino; flowering crab. Listed in nursery catalogues under its botanical name, *Malus,* not under apple.

cranberry sprays—*Ericaceae vaccinium macrocarpon* var. *V. reticulatum*. Grows in wet spots in eastern United States; also on island of Hawaii at Kilauea volcano.

crape myrtle—*Lagerstroemia indica* L.; Queen crape myrtle. Native to the Philippines, the *Lagerstroemia* species grows to over 20 feet. The split woody capsules are the joy of flower arrangers.

croton—*Codiaeum variegatum*. A tropical; bright-colored foliage, very conspicuous. Use old growth for arranging.

cryptomeria—*Cryptomeria japonica;* Japanese cedar.

cycad (or cycas)—(1) *Cycas circinalis* L.; large sago palm. The sago is not a palm, but its stiff leaves resemble palm fronds. Capable of infinite variety in arranging; (2) *C. revoluta* Thunb. A smaller variety.

cyclamen—*Cyclamen persicum* Miller. Common pink flower. To preserve flower longer, pull, do not cut, when taking it from plant. Cut off white tip on stem. Condition.

cypress—*Chamaecyparis obtusa;* Japanese cypress. See a nurseryman about other false cypresses of the *Chamaecyparis* family. Many beautiful ones, all long lasting. Coloring of needles varies.

cypripedium—*Cypripedium* Thunb. Blum; lady's slipper, *Paphiopedilum.* Lovely, small orchid with a pouch-like lip; veined; good for water-viewing style.

daffodil—*Narcissus pseudo-narcissus* L. New varieties appear every year. Use only 2 inches of water for stems in arrangements.

dahlia—*Dahlia pinnata* Cav. Never pick in bud, only full blooms; remove most leaves; char stems. Treated with these conditioning factors, flowers will last well.

daisy—(1) *Bellis perennis;* English daisy; (2) *C. frutescens* L.; marguerites; (3) shasta. *See also* gerbera daisy.

daphne—*Daphne odora* Thunb.; laurel. One of the best plants to own. Good for table paintings.

delphinium—*Delphinium ajacis* L.; larkspur. Keep hollow stems filled with water if possible.

dendrobium—*Dendrobium nobile* Lindl. Long, spray-type composed of many small flowers. Common in Hawaii; easy to grow in warm climates.

dianthus—*Dianthus caryophyllus* L. Always cut dianthus stems between the nodes for better preservation. *See also* carnation.

dieffenbachia—*Dieffenbachia picta* Schott. Easy to grow; leaves are attractive individually in arrangements. Plant is poisonous, has a peculiar odor. *See* dumbcane.

dill—*Umbelliferae: anethum graveolens.* The umbrellalike shape of the clusters of ripe seed are pretty, both fresh and dried. Attractive for holidays, sprayed gold or silver.

dock—*Polygonaceae rumex;* the buckwheat family. After flowering, stalks dry to a pretty red-brown or a golden-brown color. Considered a weed.

dollar eucalyptus—*see* eucalyptus.

dracaena—*Dracaena marginata* Lam.; marginata. A narrow, red-edged leaf. Use with its beautiful curving stem (really a trunk) which has regular, circular markings where old leaves have dropped off. Leaves cluster at the top.

dumbcane—*Dieffenbachia seguine*. Green with white spots. Called "dumbcane" because eating it causes paralysis of the tongue. *See also* dieffenbachia.

dusty meadow rue—*Thalictrum glaucum;* herb of grace. This species has a dusty, celadon-look to the leaves.

dusty miller—Several different plants are called "dusty miller." Two samples: (1) *Senecio cineraria candidissimus.* Ornamental herb; white woolly branches and leaves of a lacy pattern; (2) *A. stelleriana;* dusty miller. Gray foliage; of the sagebrush family. *See also* artemisia.

Easter lily—*Lilium longiflorum* Thunb. Try this lily with driftwood. When using the long stalk, reduce abundant leaves by one-half at least. These flowers will keep in cold storage for several weeks. *See also* lily.

echeveria—*Echeveria gilva.* Try the leaf rosettes in table painting. Succulents are easy to grow, last a long time. Give a misty spray of water frequently to aid in keeping, but do not leave any water spots on the leaves.

edgeworthia—*Edgeworthia papyrifera.* Many-branched "sticks" are most attractive. Purchase edgeworthia already dried and bleached.

enkianthus—*Enkianthus perulatus* C. K. Schn. Small, pale green leaf, dense twiggy growth, beautiful foliage.

epidendrum—*Epidendrum* sp. One of the easiest orchids to grow. Flowers cluster at the end of a long stem. All colors.

equisetum—*Equisetum hiemale.* Keep stems in shallow, not deep, water. *See also* horsetail reed.

eucalyptus—Excellent for elegant arranging; most have a pleasing, astringent aroma; all glycerinize well. (1) *E. polyanthemos;* silver dollar eucalyptus. Round or ovate gray-green leaves. (2) *E. gunnii;* cider gum. This is the longest-lasting cut eucalyptus; lasts more than a month; (3) *E. alata.* Bright scarlet fall foliage.

euonymus—(1) *Euonymus seiboldiana* Blume; spindle tree. Pale green leaves; branches will bend easily; (2) *E. japonica aureomarginata.* Spindle tree leaves edged with yellow. *See also* spindle tree.

euphorbia—*Euphorbia;* croton, poinsettia, crown of thorns, for example. A large family, most of which have a milky substance emerging when cut; the "milk" is frequently irritating to the skin. Must be conditioned carefully.

fan palm—*Livistona chinensis;* Chinese fan palm.

fatsia—*Fatsia japonica* Decne et Planch; Japanese aralia. *See also* aralia.

felt plant—*see* kalanchoe.

fern—a large family; interesting examples are: (1) *Adiantum capillis-veneris;* common maidenhair fern; (2) *Adiantiformis rumohra;* leatherleaf fern; (3) *Nephrolepis cordifolia;* common sword fern; (4) *Platycerium bifurcatum* Cav.; common staghorn fern, elkhorn fern; (5) *Stenoloma chinensis;* common lace fern. *See also* bird's nest fern.

fig—*Ficus carica;* common fig. Large diversified family.

firethorn—*see* pyracantha.

flowering almond—*Prunus amygdalis*. Blooms in early spring.

flowering apricot—*Prunus mume* Sieb et Zucc.

flowering cherry—*see* cherry.

flowering crabapple—*see* crabapple; many varieties.

flowering kale—*Brassica oleraceae;* var. *capitata* L.; ornamental kale; use in table decorations; sprinkle with water to keep it cool and fresh.

flowering peach—*see* peach.

flowering plum—*see* plum.

forsythia—*see* golden bells. A vigorous plant.

foxtail—(1) *Setaria viridis* Beauv.; bunny or fox tail; (2) *S. lutescens;* fuzzy-tailed wild grass.

fragrant olive—*see* osmanthus.

freesia—*Freesia refracta* Klatt. Fragrant flowers at the top of attractive, slender green stems.

fuchsia—Large family. Char stem ends.

funkia—*see* hosta.

gardenia—*Gardenia jasminoides* Ellis. Sweet-smelling flower; leaves and branches are attractive for arranging.

genista—*Genista monosperma;* broom.

geranium—*Pelargonium zonale* Ait. Large family.

gerbera—*Gerbera jamesonii* Bolus; Transvaal daisy. Single flower in bright colors; leaves lobed, feathery; very attractive.

giant papyrus—*see* papyrus.

giant reed—*see* reed.

ginkgo—*Ginkgoaceae ginkgo biloba;* maidenhair tree. Lovely fan-shaped leaves; male trees are ornamental.

gladiolus—*Gladiolus gandavensis* Van Houtt. One kind from a large and varied family.

gold dust leaf—*see* aucuba.

golden bells—*Forsythia suspensa* Vahl; forsythia. Force blooms on branches in early spring by cutting before leaves show and putting in water in house; in two weeks they should bloom.

golden euonymus—*see* euonymus.

gourd—*Lagenaria leucantha* Rusby, var. *gourda* Makino. Ornamental gourds.

grape—*Mahonia japonica;* holly-grape. Autumn foliage outstanding. *See also* mahonia.

great reed—*Arundo donax* L. var. *benghalensis* Makino; reed.

"ground" orchid—*see* Japanese ground orchid.

gypsophila—*see* baby's breath.

hardy orange—*Poncirus trifoliata* Rafin. Dense twiggy growth, thorny; not a real orange.

hawthorn—(1) *Crataegus cuneata* Sieb. Lovely leaves. (2) *Raphiolepis indica* Lundl.; raphiolepis. Excellent plant to own; all parts are beautiful; attributes include leaves, fruit, branching qualities, durability. An evergreen; some varieties of raphiolepis grow to 12 feet.

heather—(1) *E. calluna vulgaris;* commonly ling; (2) *E. cinerea;* heather.

heavenly bamboo—*Nandina domestica;* sacred bamboo in Japan. *See also* nandina.

heliconia—(1) *Heliconia humilis;* lobster claw. Orange-red, flattened, overlapping bracts. Common in tropical countries; (2) *H. platystachys* Baker; hanging heliconia. Red bracts edged with light green or yellow; (3) *H. psittacorum;* also called "false bird of paradise," but it is not of the bird of paradise family. Very small flower; common variety is orange; others are red.

hemp palm—*Rhapis excelsa* Thunb; bamboo palm, lady palm.

herbaceous peony—(1) *Paeonia officinalis;* common peony. Red. (2) *Paeonia albiflora;* Chinese peony. White.

hibiscus—*Hibiscus mutabilis* L. Unusually beautiful flower, but lasts only one day. Can stay out of water.

holly—(1) *Ilex integra* Thunb. Unusual holly; (2) *Ilex serrata* Thunb. Common holly with red berries; (3) *Ilex aquifolium* L. English holly with scarlet berries; (4) *Malpighia coccigera* L.; Singapore holly. Small, holly-like leaves; used in Hawaii as a substitute for holly; (5) *Osmanthus ilicifolius* Mouillef; Japanese holly. When glycerinizing holly, mash 2 inches of stem ends thoroughly before treatment. Put a piece of charcoal in the arrangement water to keep any holly arrangement fresh.

honeysuckle—(1) *Lonicera japonica* Thunb.; honeysuckle. Common; (2) *L. heckrottii* Rehd. Pink variety.

horsetail reed—*Equisetum hiemale;* equisetum.

hosta—(1) *Hosta plantaginea;* funkia or plantain lily. An improved plant of hosta; (2) *H. sieboldiana.* Blue-tinged leaves; quilted texture; (3) *H. fortunei variegata.* White-edged hosta leaf.

huckleberry—*E. Gaylussacia baccata;* whortleberry. American native huckleberry. Durable branches, small evergreen leaves.

hyacinth—*Hyacinthus orientalis* L. Fragrant, beautiful flowers on short stems. Use shallow water in arrangement container.

hydrangea—*Hydrangea macrophylla* Serenge; hydrangea. Blooms will glycerinize very well. Cut just before peak of perfection. Use only perfect flowers.

ilex—*see* holly.

iris—(1) *Iris ensata;* Japanese iris; (2) *Iris laevigata;* rabbit-ear iris. Some species of iris have orange berries in fall. Many large, beautiful flowers and leaves in this family.

ironwood—*Casuarina equisetilfolia* L. Used like pine in Hawaii and the Philippines; not a conifer, although it does have small cones.

ivy—*Hedera helix;* English ivy. Five-lobed, leathery leaf. Many varieties, some all green, some edged with white, some large, some small.

Japanese ground orchid—*Cymbidium virescens* L.; ground orchid. A variety of terrestrial orchids.

Japanese pampas grass—*Miscanthus sinensis.* A small, creamy plume. *See also* pampas.

Japanese red plum—*Prunus salicina* Lindl. One of the loveliest of spring flowering branches. Red leaves follow the flowers; *see also* plum.

Japanese yew—*Taxus cuspidata.* Stays dark green all year; red berries in autumn. *See also* yew, English.

jasmine—*see* pikake.

juniper—(1) *Juniperus chinensis;* blue vase. An evergreen with gray-green berries and bluish highlights; (2) *J. chinensis aurea.* Golden highlights; evergreen; (3) *J. virginiana;* silver spreader. Has silvery, feathery foliage, also evergreen.

Kafir corn—*G. Sorghum, vulgare.* A grain that looks like corn; grows 4 to 7 feet tall. A cylinder-shaped seed head is attractive flower material.

Kafir lily—*see* clivia.

kalanchoe—*K. beharensis* Drake; felt plant. Arrow-shaped leaves are clustered at the ends of stems. Very thick, attractive, leaves with the consistency of felt material. A succulent. For amateur gardeners, the kalanchoe family of plants is easy to grow. Nice for rock gardens as well as flower arranging.

kale—a vegetable. *See also* flowering kale.

kniphofia—*Kniphofia uvaria;* commonly, torch lily or tritoma. New varieties are constantly being developed.

koa—*Leucaena glauca; haole koa,* wild tamarind. The long koa seedpods, dried and curled, are wonderful for flower arranging for both their shape and coloring, cream and brown. Koa pods, like other seedpods, must be picked at just the proper "ripe" stage; curl each blade. Prepared clusters are available in Hawaii; look for them in flower shops. A good substitute for temperate zones is gleditsia (*Gleditschia japonica,* Miq.) seedpods.

lady palm—*see* hemp palm.

lady's slipper—*see* cypripedium.

lantana—*Lantana camara* L. Good as potted plants because they flower almost continuously. A variety of colors is available. Good for Ikebana "naturals" such as the water-viewing style. Pungent odor.

larkspur—*see* delphinium.

lauhala—the leaves of the pandanus plant; *see* pandanus.

laurel—*L. latifolia;* mountain laurel; myrtlewood. Very beautiful. Also, investigate plants of English laurel, an evergreen, *Prunus laurocerasus. See also* aucuba.

lemon leaves—*see* salal.

lemon myrtle—one of 2,800 species. *See also* myrtle, salal.

leopard flower—*see* blackberry lily.

leucothoe—*Leucothoe keiskei* Miq. Branches are important for Ikebana; leaves are leathery, durable, shiny, often bronze in winter. Grow your own leucothoe in a tub; you will always have beautiful foliage for arrangements.

liatris—*Liatris spicata* Willd. Purple-blue, spiky flowers.

ligustrum—*Ligustrum ovalifolium aureum;* golden privet. Has nice branching qualities. Use both leaves and berries.

lily—(1) *Hemerocallis flava;* yellow day lily; (2) *Gloriosa superba* L.; gloriosa lily. Strongly recurved, wavy petals. Unusual, glorious color of oranges and yellows. Stays fresh six days; (3) *Amaryllis nerine;* nerine lily. Also has deeply recurved petals; unusual coloring; (4) *Nymphaea* sp.; water lily. One of the most beautiful flowers growing. Use for *ukibana;* (5) *Lilium concolor* Salisb. var. *Buschianum* Baker; red star lily. Small, delicate, beautiful. *See also* agapanthus; amaryllis, calla.

lily turf—*Ophiopogon japonicus*. Dark green, narrow leaves to 15 inches. *See also* liriope.

lipstick plant—*see* arnotto.

liquidambar—*Liquidambar styraciflua;* American sweet gum, liquidambar. Corky branches named for their sap, a brownish, yellow gum. Buy a plant when it has its fall colors, as each tree varies.

liriope—*Liriope muscari* Bailey; lily turf. Buds are dark violet.

loquat—*Eriobotrya japonica* Lindl. Durable leaves; branching qualities very good; also has a yellow fruit that is good to eat as well as pretty. Branches glycerinize very well.

lotus—*Nelumbo nucifera* Gaertn. Seedpods are the most important part of this plant. Flowers are beautiful but fleeting, lasting only a day or so. Seedpods are a good investment for Ikebana.

lycopodium—*Lycopodium obscurum* L.; club moss. Useful in water-viewing arrangements.

magnolia—(1) *Magnolia kobus* var. *stellata;* star magnolia. Has small white flowers on bare branches; (2) *M. liliflora*. Pink or purple flowers on bare branches; (3) *M. grandiflora* L. Very large flowers. *See also* sweet bay magnolia. The evergreen leaves of any magnolia plant are fabulous; large, shiny, green on top with dark brown on the back; they glycerinize well. The flowers are spectacular. Use shallow water in vase. Flowers come before leaves in many varieties.

mahonia—*Mahonia acquifolium;* Oregon grape. Has brilliant yellow flowers and purple-blue berries. An evergreen plant. Buy one as a container plant. The foliage glycerinizes well and is unusually beautiful. *See also* grape.

mandarin orange—*Citrus deliciosa Tenore;* tangerine.

maple—(1) *Acer palmatum* Thunb.; Japanese small-leaved maple, bonfire maple. Beautiful in autumn; (2) *A. sieboldianum*. Attractive leaves for greens.

marantas—a family of beautiful leaves; not durable. *See* zigzag plant.

marguerite—*Chrysanthemum frutescens;* daisy.

marigold—*Gaillardia pulchella* Foug. Yellow and orange, long-lasting flowers. *See also* calendula.

milkweed pods—(1) *Asclepias syriaca;* common milkweed; (2) *A. tuberosa;* butterfly weed.

mitsumata—*see* edgeworthia. *Mitsumata* is a Japanese word for a commercially prepared material that is stripped of bark, treated, bleached, and often painted.

mock orange—(1) *S. philadelphus syringa;* syringa. Fragrant bloom. Airy leaf structure; (2) *P. satsumanus.* Pliable branches fine for bending.

monstera—*Monstera deliciosa* Lieb. Large, beautiful, durable leaf.

morning glory—*Ipomoea hederacea* Jacq. Fragile blue blooms.

mountain ash—*see* ash.

mulberry—*Moraceae rubra;* red mulberry. Branching characteristics are interesting in this large family. Fruits drop early, leaves wilt quickly.

mullein or mullen—(1) *Verbascum thapsus;* common mullein. Use when dried since fresh mullein tends to irritate skin. Plant has a thick, woolly stem; seeds form spiky clusters; (2) *V. cum blattaria;* moth mullein. Has small, marble-sized balls on stem. These capsules are on long, spirelike stalks, good for vertical-style arranging.

myrtle—*Myrtus communis* L. An aromatic shrub 3 to 10 feet high; has small, ovate leaves and dark blue berries. Any myrtle plant makes a good tubbed shrub for patio.

nandina—*Nandina domestica* Thunb. A favorite Ikebana material because stalks, leaves, berries, and flowers are all lovely. It is wise to grow one's own.

narcissus—*Narcissus tazetta* L. There are always new varieties of daffodils and narcissi so check with a nurseryman. Some will last two weeks as cut flowers. Use only 2 inches of water in an arrangement with narcissi.

natal plum—*see* carissa.

New Zealand flax—*Phormium tenax* Furst. Narrow, beautiful, pliable, long leaf.

night-blooming cereus—*see* cactus.

oak—*Quercus acutissima* Carruth. Use oak branches in small quantities.

okra—*Hibiscus esculentus* L.; syn. *Abelmoschus esculentus* Moench. Used as a vegetable in gumbo soup, therefore also called gumbo. Fruiting capsules, either natural or bleached, used for Ikebana. Keep them on stalks.

olive—*Oleaceae olea europaea.* All parts of this artistic tree can stimulate your creativity: bark and leaves of soft gray-green, gnarled trunk and branches, purple-black fruit. Many types.

orchid—*see* bamboo orchid; dendrobium (many species); epidendron (many species); ground orchid; cymbidium.

Oregon grape—*see* mahonia or grape.

ornithogalum—*see also* star of Bethelem. Several excellent varieties are available. White flowers.

Osage orange—*Maclura pomifera*. A rough-textured, green fruit that is most attractive; almost indestructible. Branching qualities are excellent. Not edible.

osmanthus—*Osmanthus fragrans* T. Lour.; fragrant olive. An unusually beautiful plant, first choice for a garden. Slow-growing. Cut foliage lasts more than a month.

palm—(1) *Ptychosperma macarthurii* (Wendl) Nichols; Macarthur palm. Fronds, fruits, and stems are highly ornamental; trunks are green, bamboo-like; palm "boots" (end of each palm frond) from this palm are unusually pretty; (2) *Cocos nucifera* L.; coco palm, common coconut palm. The palm "boots" (sheath of the fruit) are good containers for arranging. *See also* areca, bamboo, or hemp.

palmetto—*Sabal palmetto;* cabbage or thatch palm.

pampas grass—*Cortaderia argentea* Stapf. or *Cortaderia selloana.* Very large, long, flowing panicles, 1 to 3 feet. Stems can be 20 feet. Beautiful for both fresh and dry arrangements.

pandanus—*Pandanus variegatus* Miq.; screw pine. This pandanus has narrow green-and-white thornless leaves; excellent for Ikebana.

papyrus—(1) *Cyperus papyrus*. Beautiful, smooth, green, 3-angled stem, sometimes 5 feet in height. Papyrus half-opened, or gone to seed, are equally attractive for Ikebana. Can be spray-painted. (2) *C. isocladus* Kunth. Dwarf variety, also pleasing. Only 18 inches high.

Parrot's feather—*Myriophyllum proserpinacoides* Gill. Good for *ukibana;* a water plant. Each leaf is divided so it looks feathery.

patrinia—*Patrinia scabiosaefolia* Link.

peach—*Prunus persica* Batsch; peppermint-stick peach. Blossoms appear before leaves; a beautiful flowering branch for Ikebana.

pear—*Pyrus communis* L.; common pear. Old branches are best. Cut before flowers bloom; branches will not only blossom, but also leaf out in your arrangement.

pelargonium—*see* geranium. The geranium family is very large; all have decorative leaves. Check with a plant nursery.

peony—(1) *Paeonia suffruticosa* Andr; tree peony. *See also* herbaceous peony.

peperomia—*Peperomia sandersii* var. *argyreia* Bailey. Leaves oval-shaped; called watermelon leaves because of their characteristic stripes. Peperomias are small, attractive plants.

persimmon—*Diospyros kaki* L. Fruit branches are fun to arrange.

philadelphus—*see* mock orange.

Philippine seedpods—*Flemingia strobilifers* L.; *Favaceae; cupa cupa* in Tagalog, cereal puffs. Dry; beige or greenish-beige, triangular, puffed seedpods. A weed.

Philippine woodrose—*Merremia tuberose* L. Rendle. A cluster of seedpods in dark brown with some cream color.

philodendron—a large family of beautiful leaves.

phlox—*Phlox paniculata* L. Flowers are easy to grow.

pikake—*Jasminum sambac* L. Fragrant, small, white flowers. Double pikake resemble small white roses. Evergreen.

pine—*Pinus.* A large family, all ornamental, all long-lasting when cut. Keep one plant of the Pinus family always in your garden for cutting.

pineapple leaves—*see* ananas.

pink—*Dianthus superbus* L. Spicy-smelling, pretty flowers; small.

pitcher plant—*Nepenthes rafflesiana* Jack. A strange, insect-eating tropical.

pittosporum—*Pittosporum hosmeri* var. *longifolium.* Evergreen leaves; branches have attractive branching habits; pungent smell to a newly cut branch.

plantain lily—*see* hosta.

plum—*Prunus cistena;* dwarf red-leaf plum. *See also* flowering apricot.

plumosa fern—*see* asparagus.

podocarpus—(1) *Podocarpus chinensis* Wall; (2) *P. imbricatus* B.; *P. javanicus* Merr. Small, nail-like leaves of dark green. Both podocarpus varieties are evergreen; both are excellent for arranging.

poinsettia—*Poinsettia pulcherrima* Graham; red poinsettia. There are also creamy white and double blossom varieties.

pomegranate—(1) *Punica granatum* L. Use bare branches with one or two fruits; (2) *P.* var. *nana* L. Pers. Non-fruiting, in general, but has brilliant orange flowers that are long lasting. A dwarf form.

poppy—(1) *Papaver rhoeas* L.; (2) *P. somniferum* L.

primrose—*Primula sieboldi* Morren. Pretty, small flower.

privet—*see* ligustrum.

pussy willow—*Salix gracilistyla* Miq. Outstanding Ikebana flower material.

pyracantha—*Pyracantha angustifolia* Franch, Schneid. Angular branches bearing bright red-orange berries in fall. This plant is very thorny.

Queen Anne's lace—*Daucus catrota* L.; wild carrot. A weed, but a most attractive, lacy one.
quince—*Chaenomeles lagenaria* Koidz; Japanese flowering quince.

ranunculus—*Ranunculaceae*. Buttercup family; a camellia-type, flat flower. Not too hardy, but beautiful colors.
raphiolepis—*see* hawthorn.
rattan—*Calamus discolor* Mart. A climbing palm. Young plants are commonly used as potted plants. Stalks are attractive.
redbud—*Cercus chinensis*. Bare branches have flowers in early spring.
red castorbean—*see* castorbean.
reed, giant—*Arundo donax* var. *versicolor* Miller. A perennial grass; leaves striped with white in this variety.
rhododendron—*Rhododendron metternichii*. One variety of a large family that includes trailing arbutus, wintergreen, mountain laurel, heather, and the azaleas. Hybrids are multiple. The majority of rhododendrons are evergreens; they take glycerine well. Shop for a favorite.
rhubarb—*Rheum rhaponticum;* pie plant. Check for any new species developed recently.
rohdea—(1) *Rohdea japonica;* sacred lily of China. Dark green leaves; good pot plant; (2) *R. marginata*. Long, stiff, dark green leaves with yellow edges. Decorative red berries on both varieties.
rose—large family from which to choose.
rubber plant—(1) *Ficus elastica;* India rubber tree. Many interesting small trees in the fig family; (2) *F. lyrata;* fiddleleaf.

safflower—*Carthamus tinctorius*. Flower and seedpod dry well.
sago palm—*see* cycad.
salal—*Gaultheria shallon*. Lemon leaves; long-lasting, fragrant.
salvia—*Salvia coccinea* L.; sage. Salvia is a poker-shaped flower.
sansevieria—(1) *Sansevieria thyrsiflora* Thunb.; mother-in-law tongue, snake plant, spear plant. This variety is the common, dull green, grayish cross stripes; (2) *S. trifasciata* var. *laurentii*. Fleshy leaves have yellow, vertical bands, nice natural curves; (3) *S. cylindrica* Bojer. 1-inch thick, long, cylindrical columns, like large, long crayons. Same characteristic gray-green color.
Scotch broom—*see* broom.
sea coral (sea fan)—not vegetable, but animal. Lovely colors and shapes formed by millions of tiny animals called coral polyps add beauty, color, and imagination to your creative arrange-

ments. You will be particularly enchanted with the lacy sea fan from the West Indies or South Pacific waters. Your florist wholesaler will have them in yellow, rose, purple-brown, and maybe even in black. They may be spray-painted to match your decor of the moment. Good points to know about sea fans: (1) If they are ragged and need trimming, use a pair of heavy shears and trim carefully to shape; (2) They will curve if you wet them; wire them in place, then dry.

sea grape—*Coccoloba uvifera* L. Jacq. Ornamental, interesting, flat, circular leaves of gray-green but veined in red. Sea-grape jelly made from red fruit is good; fruit is not usable in arranging—it is too soft. Twisting branches.

shasta daisy—*see* daisy.

silver tree—*Leucadendron argenteum*. The foliage is silky, of a silvery green color; very handsome. Leaves keep two weeks.

skunk cabbage—*Symplocarpus foetidus*. Convoluted leaves with beautiful coloring when young. No smell when young.

slipper flower—*see* zigzag plant.

snapdragon—*Antirrhinum majus* L. Tall, spiky flowers, common.

snow willow—*see* spiraea.

Solomon's seal—*Polygonatum lasianthum* Maxim. Green-and-white durable leaf.

spice tree—*M. pimenta officinalis;* allspice. An evergreen of the myrtle family. Aromatic leaves.

spider grass plant—*Chlorophytum comosum* Thunb; airplane plant. Good for table-painting arrangements. Easy to grow in pots.

spindle tree—(1) *Euonymous japonica*. All green leaves. (2) *E. alatus;* winged spindle tree. Corky flanges on branches. *See also* euonymous.

spiraea—*S. thunbergii;* snow willow. Tiny white flowers, small leaves on graceful branches. *See also* bridal wreath.

spruce—*Picea jezoensis* Carr.; a variety of blue spruce.

staghorn fern—*see* fern.

star of Bethlehem—*Ornithogalum umbellatum;* ornithogalum. The hardy flower keeps for weeks. You should grow one of this variety in your garden.

statice—*Limonium* sp., see lavender. Large group, perennial herbs. Dry well. Species range from stalky-type stems to lacy branching types. Prettiest color is a deep blue lavender variety.

stock—*Matthiola incana* R. Br. A beautiful flower in cream, white, or lavender, which needs lots of water to survive well. Clean underwater stems of leaves carefully or they will rot quickly and become unpleasant smelling.

strawflower—*C. Helichrysum bracteatum*. Everlasting.

strelitzia—*see* bird of paradise.

sugar cane—*Saccharum officinarum*. Several varieties; some have yellow-striped, or red, or green stalks. Flowering cane plumes are most ornamental.

sumac or sumach—(1) *Rhus javanica* L. Sumac; (2) *Rhus hirta;* staghorn sumac; (3) *R. copallina* Miq.; dwarf sumac. Poison sumac white berries always grow in drooping clusters. Avoid these types. Red berries are upright.

sunflower—*Helianthus annus* L. Large, yellow, flat blooms. Dries in interesting, contorted shapes.

sweet alyssum—*C. Lobularia maritima*. Small, clustered flowers, easy to grow.

sweet bay magnolia—*Magnolia virginiana*. Has an interesting calyx. Preserve it.

sweet pea—*Lathyrus odoratus* L. Dainty, fragrant flowers.

sweet william—*Dianthus barbatus* L. Keeps well; easy to grow.

sword-brake—*Pteris ensiformis* var. *victoriae*. White-striped sword brake. Try in water-viewing style.

syringa—*see* mock orange.

tamarind—*see* koa.

tangerine—*Rutaceae citrus deliciosa* Tenore; mandarin orange. Excellent size for use in *morimono* arrangements.

tansy—(1) *Tanacetum vulgare*. Common, small flower, dainty; (2) *T. huronense*. Can be preserved dry.

teasel—*Dipsacus fullonum*. Many types of teasels. Weeds. Use them in dry state.

thistle—(1) *Cirsium japonicum* D.C. Japanese use this as a fresh flower; small, lavender-pink in color; (2) *C. salvia carduacea;* thistle sage. Use these white, woolly, spiny flowers when they are old, not fresh. Quite attractive when spray-painted gold; (3) *Compositae liatrias;* star thistle, blazing star. A pestlike tumbleweed, blazing star has stiff, gray stems with bristly seed heads. All thistles are prickly but attractive and long-lasting in arrangements. Use the last two above in dry form.

ti—*Cordyline terminalis* L. Ornamental varieties abound. Fruits of *ti* (pronounced tee) are as attractive as the leaves.

tiger grass—*see* broom.

tiger lily—*Lilium tigrinum;* common garden lily.

tillandsia—*Tillandsia lindeniana*. A bromeliad with flower spikes formed by overlapping bracts. Bromeliads belong to the pineapple family and deserve your attention if you like long-lasting flowers. Dwarf bromeliads can be grown on a piece of driftwood as attractive house plants.

tree peony—*see* peony.

tritoma—*see* kniphofia.

tuberose—*Polianthes tuberosa* L. An extremely fragrant stalk of white flowers used often for weddings. Avoid bruising the petals.

tulip—*Tulipa gesneriana* L. Common garden plant. Check new varieties; some have fringed edges.

tumbleweed—also known as Russian thistle. Common in large areas of North America.

uki grass—Cladium leptostachyum; *uki* in Hawaiian, volcano or Pele grass. Long, slender stalks of cream color have dark brown, wheat-type flowering tops. Available dry.

umbrella grass—*Cyperus alternifolius* L.; umbrella plant or Japanese umbrella plant. Leafless. Ornamental for water gardens; extremely attractive with its long, slender green stem.

variegated giant reed—*see* reed.

variegated laurel—*see* aucuba.

violet—*Viola mandshurica* W. Beck. Common. Used massed rather than only single stems.

volcano grass—see *uki* grass.

water lily—*see* lily. Water lilies are called "sleeping flowers" by the Japanese because for two or three days they open every morning and close every afternoon. Water-lily hybrids come in different colors; some open at different times of the day or night.

wheat—locate dry wheat stems in florist shops; inexpensive. Fresh, pale green, new wheat is available in season in Japan; perhaps it may also be found in your community.

willow—(1) *Salix babylonica* L.; weeping willow. Cut branches three weeks before you need them. Strip all leaves, and put in water. After three weeks, new fresh leaves will appear for a beautiful arrangement; (2) *S. gracilistyla;* pussy willow; (3) *S. sachalinense Sekka;* fasciated or twisted willow; (4) *S. matsudana tortuosa;* dragon willow or corkscrew willow.

winterberry—*Ilex verticillata. See also* holly.

wistaria—*Wistaria floribunda* D. C.; wistaria vine. Fresh flowers hold only one day. Use dry, bleached, flexible stems.

woodrose—(1) *Operculina tuberosa.* Large, single seed capsules for flower arranging. Hawaii and the Philippines; (2) *Argyreia nervosa;* baby woodroses. Woolly or silver morning glory. Clustered seed capsules are beautiful in cream and dark brown.

yarrow—*Achillea sibirica* Ledeb. Flowers hold their dark yellow color well when dried. Remove all leaves.

yellow day lily—*Hemerocallis disticha* Do.

yellow pond lily—*Nuphar japonicum;* fragile lily. Lasts only a few hours.

yew, English—*Taxus baccata.* Dark green, small-leafed, hardy plant. Red berries. *See also* Japanese yew.

yucca—*Yucca gloriosa* L.; Spanish bayonet; God's candlesticks. Flowering stalks good for exhibitions because they are so large, often over 3 feet. For smaller arrangements, cut flowering stalks apart. Stiff, leathery leaves, long-lasting, rigid; sharp spines.

zebra plant—*Calathea zebrina* Lindl.; syn. *Maranta zebrina* Sims. Zebra plant is so called because of the dark green stripes on the green leaves. Flowers are inconspicuous, but leaves are unusually beautiful.

zigzag plant—*Pedilanthus tithymaloides;* slipper flower. White-bordered, milky; angled growth pattern to stems gives the plant its common name. Variety called *variegata Hort.* has curled leaves.

zinnia—*Zinnia elegans* L. Easy to grow; attractive flowers with little effort. Flowers last well if picked in full bloom. Take a bucket of water to the garden in which to place freshly cut stems.

Glossary

art of elimination: knowing where to remove excess from a piece of flower material to achieve maximum beauty

base (for flower arrangement): any specially designed unit upon which a flower composition sits; usually made of wood

bulk: the physical amount of space a flower material or vase occupies in an arrangement

cascading pattern: a flowing design for a flower arrangement

centerpiece: a five-sided flower arrangement (four sides and the top)

chabana: a sparse Japanese flower arrangement made specifically for the Japanese tea-ceremony room

Character flower arrangement: a term used by this author to designate an arrangement that combines Ikebana and Western flower arranging

clay-in: to fasten a pinholder firmly into a container with floral clay

conditioning: filling cells of freshly cut plant material with water to preserve freshness

container: any receptacle for a flower composition; one of the three basic elements of a flower arrangement

cross-bar holder: two small sticks inserted cross-shaped into the mouth of a tall vase to hold flower material

cup pinholder: a needlepoint holder encased in a metal "cup" that will hold water

depth: a three-dimensional factor that gives "distance" to an Ikebana

driftwood: any wood drifting in or washed up by ocean, lake, or mountain stream

dry material: flower material that needs no water

exotica: flower material not usually native to the arranger's locale

floral picks: small, pointed, wooden sticks with a thin wire attached for supporting slender flower stalks

floral tape: an elasticized, thin, papery adhesive used to mask the mechanics of wiring

florist wire: short lengths of wire available in various gauges

glycerinizing: preserving fresh flower material so that it stays soft, pliable, similar to its original state

growth pattern: characteristic branching or shape of any flower material

hanging arrangement: a suspended composition hung from a unit attached to the ceiling or a fixture fastened to a wall

horizontal design: an arrangement built on a near-parallel line to the rim of a container

Ikebana: a Japanese term normally translated as the art of Japanese flower arranging

kenzan: Japanese word for needlepoint holder

manipulation: curving, bending, or cutting flower material into rhythmic contours

mobile flower-sculptures: creative arrangements hung from a chain, nylon cording, or string, allowing the unit to move freely with air currents

morimono: an Ikebana-style arrangement using fruit, vegetables, flowers, bulbs, roots

needlepoint holder: an assembly of needlelike steel pins on a lead-mixture base; unusually heavy for its size

Oasis: a trade name for a water-holding compound; manufactured foam

orchid tube: a small, plastic tube with a flexible rubber top for holding one flower in water (florists use these tubes for single orchids)

Peacock pattern: a design built on the radiating lines of a peacock's tail or fan

perspective: a three-dimensional element of Ikebana

plastic foam: a man-made product of three types: (1) Oasis, for holding fresh flower stems in water; (2) Styrofoam, for holding dry flower stems; (3) foam made into various shapes to use as accents in the arrangement proper

pliability: a capability of some plant materials to form rhythmic patterns under proper hand pressures

preservation: a process of (1) preserving "permanent" materials; (2) prolonging the life of fresh flowers through conditioning

sculpturing: any creative shaping, cutting, handling, or assembling of flower materials into an original design

setting or positioning: one of the three basic elements in achieving a perfect flower arrangement

shikibana: *see* table painting

stabilize: to balance a flower material firmly in an arrangement

Styrofoam: *see* plastic foam

table painting: an arrangement without container, holder, or water, laid directly on the table; *shikibana* in Japanese

texture: the surface appearance and detail of any piece of flower material

three-dimensionality: Japanese achievement in flower placement which gives a natural impression of depth through the use of space and perspective

tokonoma: a Japanese floor-to-ceiling niche used to display family art treasures and Ikebana

transpiration: the evaporation of water from leaves

ukibana: "floating flower"; one style of Ikebana in which flowers float in water

usubata: one of several types of Japanese bronze containers used in formal arrangements

vertical design: upright, dramatic pattern for a flower arrangement

visual weight: the amount of attention the eye gives to a specific part of a flower composition

water painting: flowers laid on or near the surface of the water in a container; see also *ukibana*

Bibliography

Berrall, Julia S.: *A History of Flower Arrangement*, rev. ed., Viking Press, New York, 1968

Carr, Rachel E.: *Japanese Floral Art: Symbolism, Cult and Practice*, D. Van Nostrand, New York, 1961

————: *Creative Ways with Flowers*, Doubleday, Garden City, N.Y., 1970

Conway, Gregory J.: *Encyclopedia of Flower Arrangement*, Alfred A. Knopf, New York, 1957

Hirsch, Sylvia: *Art of Table Setting and Flower Arrangement*, 2nd ed., T. Y. Crowell, New York, 1967

Ikenobo, Sen'ei: *Ikebana: Nageire and Moribana*, Nihon Kado-sha, Kyoto, 1962

————: *Ikebana*, Hoikusha, Osaka, 1966

Kasuya, Meikof: *Imaginative Ikebana*, Japan Publications, Tokyo 1970

Li, H. L.: *Chinese Flower Arrangement*, Hedera House, Philadelphia, 1956

Neal, Marie C.: *In Gardens of Hawaii*, Lancaster Press, Lanchester, Pa., 1956

Nichols, Beverley: *The Art of Flower Arrangement*, Viking Press, New York, 1967

Ohara, Houn: *Creation with Flowers*, Kodansha International, Tokyo, 1966

————: *Ikebana: The Creative Tradition*, Kodansha International, Tokyo, 1969

Ohno, Noriko: *Creative Ikebana*, Japan Publications, Tokyo, 1969

Oshikawa, Josui: *Manual of Japanese Flower Arrangement*, Kokusai Kado Kaikan, Tokyo, 1959

Oshikawa, Josui, and Gorham, Hazel H.: *Manual of Japanese Flower Arrangement*, Cultural Exchange Club, Tokyo, 1951

Reister, Dorothy W.: *Design for Flower Arrangers,* D. Van Nostrand, Princeton, 1959

Sparnon, Norman J.: *Japanese Flower Arrangement: Classical and Modern,* Charles E. Tuttle, Rutland, Vermont and Tokyo, 1960

———: *The Poetry of Leaves,* John Weatherhill, Tokyo, 1970

———: *Ikebana with Roses,* Shufunotomo, Tokyo, 1972

Steiner, Mona Lisa: *Philippine Ornamental Plants and Their Care,* 2nd ed., Carmelo and Bauerman, Manila, 1960

Stoltz, Mrs. Raymond R.: *Interpretive Floral Designs,* A. S. Barnes, South Brunswick, N. J., 1972

Teshigahara, Kasumi: *Space and Color,* Kodansha International, Tokyo 1965

Teshigahara, Sofu: *Sofu: His Boundless World of Flowers and Form,* Kodansha International, Tokyo, 1966

———: *The Art of Mr. Sofu,* Ikebana, vol. 2, Shufunotomo, Tokyo, 1971

Thompson, Mary E.: *The Driftwood Book,* 2nd ed., D. Van Nostrand, New York, 1966

Index